If you are ready to tackle emotions that m
vibrant life beyond trauma, Carolyn B. All
Your Guilt and Shame, will lead you there. T
and warmth in her words. The writing exercises and case examples of real
people make this book a pocket coach for deep and lasting healing. We all
deserve to feel just a little bit better!

—REBECCA E. WILLIAMS, PhD, PSYCHOLOGIST, WELLNESS EXPERT,
AND AWARD-WINNING SELF-HELP AUTHOR; AUTHOR OF *SIMPLE WAYS TO
UNWIND WITHOUT ALCOHOL: 50 TIPS TO DRINK LESS AND ENJOY MORE*

If you struggle with guilt and shame, this book is a must-read. Dr. Allard has
compiled her years of expertise as a trauma specialist into an accessible and
transformational guide. The case examples and exercises will have you understanding and letting go of your guilt and shame, all while connecting to and
living your most deeply held personal values. I highly recommend this book!

—JILL STODDARD, PhD, AUTHOR OF *IMPOSTER NO MORE, BE MIGHTY,*
AND *THE BIG BOOK OF ACT METAPHORS*

Dr. Carolyn B. Allard offers a clear and compassionate path forward from guilt
and shame after trauma. Through rich examples and helpful exercises, Allard
explores the roots of guilt and shame and explains science-backed steps for
healing in a resource that will be invaluable to survivors and clinicians.

—ANNE P. DePRINCE, PhD, AUTHOR OF *EVERY 90 SECONDS:
OUR COMMON CAUSE ENDING VIOLENCE AGAINST WOMEN*

Given the high prevalence of PTSD in the general population and the large
numbers of PTSD patients who seek psychotherapy, this book is a milestone
on the road to a more complete treatment for trauma and PTSD.

—TERENCE M. KEANE, PhD, ASSOCIATE CHIEF OF STAFF FOR RESEARCH, VA
BOSTON HEALTHCARE SYSTEM; DIRECTOR, BEHAVIORAL SCIENCE DIVISION,
NATIONAL CENTER FOR POSTTRAUMATIC STRESS DISORDER; PROFESSOR OF
PSYCHIATRY & ASSISTANT DEAN FOR RESEARCH, CHOBANIAN AND AVEDISIAN
SCHOOL OF MEDICINE AT BOSTON UNIVERSITY, BOSTON, MA

In this compassionate and wise guide, Carolyn B. Allard lays out a road map for healing from guilt and shame. Based on her years of clinical experience and her deep knowledge of research, Allard provides specific and practical healing activities from which readers will find hope and a way forward.

–JENNIFER JOY FREYD, PhD, PROFESSOR EMERIT, PSYCHOLOGY, UNIVERSITY OF OREGON, EUGENE, OR

Carolyn B. Allard translates her years of expertise working with trauma survivors into a user-friendly guide to manage guilt and shame and move through trauma to thrive in life. An excellent companion for those struggling after experiencing trauma.

–SHEILA A. M. RAUCH, PhD, ABPP, MARK AND BARBARA KLEIN DISTINGUISHED PROFESSOR, DEPARTMENT OF PSYCHIATRY AND BEHAVIORAL SCIENCES, EMORY UNIVERSITY SCHOOL OF MEDICINE, ATLANTA, GA

We may understand that guilt and shame bring us much suffering, but unless we have the tools to identify and transform these nonadaptive guilt and shame thoughts, we are stuck in this misery. Dr. Allard has written a comprehensive, accessible book that gives us the road map to develop a realistic view of our past trauma and adversity with clarity and compassion.

–BHIKSHUNI THUBTEN JIGME, BUDDHIST NUN, SRAVASTI ABBEY, NEWPORT, WA

In many years of doing trauma work with clients, it has become apparent that resulting guilt and shame from trauma are what people struggle with most and what keeps them stuck in their lives. This book is exactly what is needed to provide applicable ways that people can address and resolve guilt and shame and get their lives back!

–EBONY BUTLER, PhD, COUNSELING PSYCHOLOGY, THE CENTER FOR CREATING CHANGE, ATLANTA, GA; CREATOR OF MY THERAPY CARDS®

TRANSFORM
Your Guilt
and Shame

TRANSFORM
Your Guilt
and Shame

Evidence-Based Strategies to Heal
From Trauma and Adversity

CAROLYN B. ALLARD, PhD, ABPP

 AMERICAN PSYCHOLOGICAL ASSOCIATION

Published by
American Psychological Association
750 First Street, NE
Washington, DC 20002
https://www.apa.org

Order Department
https://www.apa.org/pubs/books
order@apa.org

Typeset in Sabon by Circle Graphics, Inc., Reisterstown, MD

Printer: Gasch Printing, Odenton, MD
Cover Designer: Mark Karis
Cover Art: Origami idea inspired by Donatienne Foltz.

Library of Congress Cataloging-in-Publication Data

Names: Allard, Carolyn B. (Carolyn Brigitte), 1968- author.
Title: Transform your guilt and shame : evidence-based strategies to heal
    from trauma and adversity / authored by Carolyn B. Allard.
Description: Washington, DC : American Psychological Association, [2025] |
    Includes bibliographical references and index.
Identifiers: LCCN 2024013515 (print) | LCCN 2024013516 (ebook) |
    ISBN 9781433843419 (paperback) | ISBN 9781433843426 (ebook)
Subjects: LCSH: Guilt. | Shame. | Psychic trauma--Treatment. | BISAC:
    SELF-HELP / Emotions | SELF-HELP / Self-Management / Stress Management
Classification: LCC BF575.G8 A528 2025 (print) | LCC BF575.G8 (ebook) |
    DDC 152.4/4--dc23/eng/20240517
LC record available at https://lccn.loc.gov/2024013515
LC ebook record available at https://lccn.loc.gov/2024013516

https://doi.org/10.1037/0000419-000

Printed in the United States of America

10 9 8 7 6 5 4 3 2 1

CONTENTS

TRANSFORM
Your Guilt
and Shame

HOW TO USE THIS BOOK

Are you trapped in an unending spiral of guilt or shame about something bad that happened? Do you beat yourself up with thoughts that you are responsible, you are to blame, you could and should have done something different to prevent it from happening or to make things better faster? Do you feel like you did something that went against your values or morals or were not justified in doing what you did? Do you believe that something must be wrong with you, you deserve to have bad things happen, you are not worthy of forgiveness, or you are not entitled to feel better? If so, this book may be for you.

THE EFFECTS OF UNHEALTHY GUILT AND SHAME

Guilt and shame are two of the most painful emotions we can experience. In fact, guilt and shame are so aversive that they compel us to do things, anything, to avoid feeling them. You may do this by distracting yourself with other activities to avoid thinking about the events you feel guilt or shame about, trying to numb the feelings with substances, getting defensive and blaming other people to avoid feeling shame, or sinking into depression and deciding not to show your face anywhere that might remind you of the events or your feelings. Regardless of what strategy you use, even if you have gotten good at not feeling your emotions some of the time or even most of the time, shame and guilt may still rear their ugly heads and wreak havoc in your life.

Another way you may try to cope with guilt and shame may be more counterintuitive. You may actively remind yourself of your guilt and shame in the hopes that by constantly feeling bad about yourself, you can keep yourself in check. In other words, you may beat yourself up to overcompensate for any past mistakes to avoid feeling more guilt and shame in the future.

Most people who suffer from guilt and shame tend to go back and forth between these two extremes, sometimes avoiding their feelings and other times overfocusing on them. Either way keeps you stuck in a negative, self-perpetuating loop of guilt and shame that just makes these feelings more intense, distressing, and difficult to cope with. This loop is called the nonadaptive guilt and shame cycle, or NAGS cycle.

As if being stuck in this cycle of increasingly distressing emotions is not painful enough, it can cause other problems, such as the following:

- overreacting to situations
- feeling out of control
- needing to know everything or have control over everything to feel safe
- poor self-esteem
- anxiety, which can include worrying, feeling on edge or on guard, feeling jumpy, and being easily startled
- depression, which can include feeling sad or down most of the time, having little energy, and not being able to feel any positive emotions or enjoy things, even things you used to enjoy
- physical problems such as headaches or migraines, muscle aches, rapid heart rate, shallow breathing, fidgetiness, sweating, dry mouth, or stomach and gastrointestinal issues

- intrusive thoughts or feelings about past events
- difficulty concentrating or remembering things
- relationship problems, such as not being able to trust or get close to anyone, not being able to feel love, feeling like others will judge you negatively, having difficulty asking for what you need, having poor boundaries, or being passive or aggressive or passive-aggressive
- irritability, angry outbursts, short temper, and aggressiveness
- reliance on unhealthy coping methods such as substances, gambling, sex or pornography, sweets or other unhealthy comfort foods, high-risk activities like extreme sports, shopping, video gaming, and social media
- difficulty with daily living activities, such as eating, sleeping, exercising, and attending to personal hygiene

In this book, you will learn how to stop the unhealthy guilt and shame loop that contributes to these problems. Furthermore, you will learn how to use guilt and shame constructively. Together, these strategies will help you regain a sense of control over your life. Just imagine being able to feel safe and comfortable around others, going about your day-to-day business without feeling like there's something wrong with you or assuming other people think there's something wrong with you, and being able to make choices that are in line with your values rather than reacting reflexively in ways you later regret. These are the outcomes people report after undergoing the therapy on which the strategies in this book are based.

MY BACKGROUND AND APPROACH TO TREATING NAGS

What makes me an expert on guilt and shame? I am a board-certified licensed clinical psychologist with over 25 years of experience providing direct clinical care, training, and consultation on trauma and guilt and conducting research on these topics. In my experience with hundreds of therapy clients and research participants, I have personally witnessed the havoc that guilt and shame can wreak on trauma survivors and those around them. Together with other trauma experts, I developed a therapy called trauma informed guilt reduction (TrIGR), which has been shown in scientific studies to reduce unhealthy guilt and shame and symptoms of posttraumatic stress disorder (PTSD), depression, and general distress. My colleagues and I have continued to see firsthand the benefit of addressing guilt and shame in the therapy room using TrIGR.

This book provides you with the same information and strategies you would be taught by a therapist in TrIGR therapy. TrIGR is a form of cognitive behavior therapy, which is the most scientifically supported therapy for many mental health conditions. It involves identifying and changing problematic ways of thinking (cognition) and acting (behavior). Like clients in TrIGR therapy, you will learn ways to catch and change some of the ways you have come to think and act that induce problematic guilt and shame. You will learn that while you are not responsible for being in a NAGS cycle, you can be responsible for getting out of it. You will learn how to transform your life-hijacking guilt and shame into life-enhancing feelings and to live a life in which you take hold of the reins—in which you can make choices according to your values and morals instead of your reflexive survival system.

SET YOURSELF UP FOR SUCCESS

Before you start, I want to provide you with some ways you can set yourself up for success. These proven strategies for changing behavior or developing new habits are supported by the latest psychological science.

- **Do the exercises.** What you get out of this book mostly depends on what you do with it. The book provides strategies that help you confront problematic thoughts, but you have to use the strategies, not just read about them. Thus, I have provided several written exercises for you to practice the strategies. Please take the time to complete these exercises. Writing your thoughts down helps you examine them more objectively, which helps you challenge them and, if needed, convert them into beneficial ones. You are worth the time and effort. You are provided with worksheets you can directly write on throughout the book. If you prefer to write on separate pieces of paper or use digital worksheets, you can download free versions of the worksheets from https://www.apa.org/pubs/books/transform-your-guilt-shame (see the Resources tab).
- **Practice, practice, practice.** By "practice," I mean read this book and do the exercises. Just as repetition is essential for learning new skills, it will be helpful for you to read and follow the guidance for each strategy in the following chapters more than once. If you're like most people, your mind harbors more than one reason you should feel guilt and shame. That means you will probably have good reason to go through each step more than once to address each version of guilt and shame conclusions you have come to. In addition, some instances of guilt and shame are particularly sticky and will benefit from being addressed more than once using the strategies in this book.
- **Block off reading and practice times in your schedule.** Try scheduling an hour a couple of times a week. If that doesn't seem feasible, start smaller: 30 minutes on 1 day this week. The more time you can commit to practicing and the more consistently you do it, the quicker you will notice positive changes. But it's better that you start with some time (and some benefit) than with no time (and no benefit). Also, identify alternate times that you

could read and practice in case something unexpected happens and you can't when you intended to.

- **Pick a time when you are alert.** Some mood or mind-altering substances interfere with our capacity to learn and benefit from any practice we might do. These include alcohol, recreational drugs, or certain doses of prescription medications, such as those that have a sedative, muscle-relaxing, or quick-acting anxiety reduction effect (e.g., anxiolytics, benzodiazepines, tranquilizers, barbiturates, beta-blockers, sedatives, muscle relaxants, sleep medications). So, pick a time when these substances are not in your system.

- **Pick a place where you will be most productive and make it as distraction free as possible.** Minimize your access to anything you find especially entertaining, distracting, or addictive. For example, some of my clients find it helpful to put their phones on silent or airplane mode, and they try not to be in a room where they normally access social media, television, video games, alcohol, drugs, or food. It's also helpful if you cannot see any of the work or house chores you have to do. You may have noticed that sometimes, even things you don't normally consider fun will suddenly seem compelling when you are trying to do something new or challenging.

- **Set reminders or alarms for your practice times.** Don't wait until you feel like reading or practicing the skills (chances are you won't). Just do it when you've scheduled the time to do it. Here are some suggestions my clients have shared with me: Put up some sticky notes in places you tend to see or touch during the times of day you have scheduled to practice your new habits (e.g., on the coffee machine for your first thing in the morning practice time); set a reminder on your alarm clock, smartphone, computer, smart speaker, or other programmable tech gadget; keep your practice reminders and notes in a prominent place (e.g., on your desk, kitchen counter, or coffee table) and not filed away in a cabinet or drawer or under stacks of other papers or clutter.

- **Block off whatever time you need before your scheduled practice time to make sure you will be ready to start on time with no impediments or interruptions.** For example, you might need to eat, get yourself a glass of water, get access to your book and what you need to take notes, let others know that you are not going to be available during that time, drop the kids off with the neighbors, go to your most productive place, and clear your space and hide things that can distract you. You might set an alarm to remind yourself to do that, too.

- **Set another alarm for the end of your practice time so you can focus on what you're doing instead of checking the time.** You could even set an alarm 10 minutes before the end of your scheduled practice time so you have a heads up and can wrap up what you are working on. If you don't have enough time to start and finish a new section, you could review and reflect on what you just did instead. Remember that repetition is a good thing.

- **Reward yourself.** We are more likely to keep doing something if it is reinforced. So, reward yourself after doing anything you planned on doing during your scheduled practice time. This does not have to be extravagant or take much time or money. You could just go outside or to a window and let the sun warm your face while you smile at what you have accomplished, eat that piece of chocolate you have been keeping for a special occasion, take a luxurious bath, prepare yourself a soothing tea, listen to your favorite music and sing aloud or dance your heart out, call a friend who makes you laugh, brag to someone who will be happy to hear what you have done so far in this process, go for a walk, or just sit in a beautiful place outside. It does not matter what the reward is or how big or small it is, as long as it is pleasant to you. It's not a bad idea to make a list of pleasant things ahead of time and even schedule rewarding activities after each scheduled practice session to increase the chance that you will reward yourself and, therefore, increase the chance you will continue with the work of developing your new habits to interrupt your problematic guilt and shame loop.

What you are attempting to do by following these tips is to make it as hard as possible not to follow through with doing what you set out to do.

OVERVIEW OF THE BOOK

Chapter 1 is a primer on guilt and shame. My aim is to share with you what the latest research says about why we have guilt and shame, how they can serve us well, and how they can go awry and cause problems like the ones you are experiencing. Many people report that having this background information is useful. It helps them better appreciate where their guilt and shame come from, which often helps folks at least stop feeling more guilt and shame for feeling guilt and shame in the first place. You will learn that there are good reasons people come to inaccurate conclusions of guilt to survive adversity, and you will learn the traps our minds can fall into that lead us to faulty perspectives under certain circumstances. This information also makes clear that when guilt and shame no longer serve you well, you can change them from distressing and unhelpful emotions into more beneficial ones.

Equipped with this information, in Chapter 2, you will be led through a series of tips and questions to help you identify the thoughts contributing to your nonadaptive guilt and shame. These thoughts can be divided into five categories or types of conclusions: foreseeability and preventability, insufficient justification, responsibility, wrongdoing, and violated values. In Chapters 3 through 7, you will learn to challenge each of these types of conclusions. In each case, you will be provided with step-by-step instructions and examples of how you can come to more accurate and, therefore, more helpful perspectives.

Once you learn to challenge the types of thoughts that lead to nonadaptive guilt and shame, you can start using your new, more positive outlook to guide your future actions. Chapter 8 will teach you how to use your past and future feelings of guilt and shame to identify your values—what is important to you. And you will use values as guideposts to start building the kind of life you want to live, in which you hold the reins and can choose to engage in things that are important to you—a life that has meaning.

In the Afterword, I provide advice to ensure you continue to benefit from all the effort you have exerted. The strategies in this book are powerful; the more you use them, the more positive impact they will have.

Finally, if you are interested, there are appendixes with additional resources and references. In Appendix A, you will find an extra copy of each worksheet provided throughout the book. You can also download free versions of the worksheets from https://www.apa.org/pubs/books/transform-your-guilt-shame (see the Resources tab). Appendix B offers guidance for finding other reliable resources that might be helpful to you. Challenging your guilt and shame using the strategies in this book will help address some of your problems, but there are many other effective tools and resources that could assist you with various mental health and behavioral challenges that are outside the scope of this book. Appendix C lists references to all the scientific evidence supporting the information and strategies presented in the book.

CASE EXAMPLES

Throughout the book, I provide specific and real examples from my professional and personal experiences to help illustrate concepts and different ways to implement the strategies. For each of the client examples I introduce here, I intentionally selected individuals diverse in age, race and ethnicity, gender and sexual identity, ability, socioeconomic status, religion, and country of origin. To help maintain confidentiality, some of these details have been omitted or changed, and no real names were used. In some cases, the particulars of different actual clients have been combined into a composite character.

- **Saj,** a woman of Indian descent, was emotionally and physically abused by her wife for over 10 years before she was able to leave at the age of 41.
- **Duri,** a 44-year-old nonbinary Korean American, survived a devastating earthquake while volunteering abroad that killed hundreds and displaced thousands.
- **Maxwell,** a 27-year-old White veteran of the Iraq war, nearly lost his life when a rocket-propelled grenade exploded inches in front of him on a busy street, killing many civilians and fellow service members.
- **Charmaine,** a Black 64-year-old woman, was sexually abused by a close family friend in childhood and sexually assaulted outside a bar as a young adult. There was physical violence involved in the assault she experienced in adulthood but not when she was abused as a child.
- **Felipe** was the 21-year-old son of indigenous Guatemalan immigrants who was teased, called names, and socially ostracized by his peers at school for years after moving in his early teens to a small town that had few people of color.

These individuals are discussed throughout the book to illustrate the techniques for addressing problematic guilt and shame. Whether or not you relate to their specific adverse circumstances, you will likely relate to the types of thinking that trapped them in nonadaptive guilt and shame (or NAGS). You will see them confront and transform their guilt and shame and, hopefully, this will inspire you to apply the same principles to your situation. Now, let's get started!

CHAPTER I

THE CYCLE OF NONADAPTIVE GUILT AND SHAME

Let's begin by defining guilt and shame, and later in the chapter we will see how trauma and adversity can lead to an unhealthy guilt and shame spiral. The terms *guilt* and *shame* are often used interchangeably, which makes sense because these two experiences are related and often co-occur. But they are somewhat different. Guilt refers to what we experience when we feel distress about something we have done—a behavior. For example, let's say my best friend tells me it would mean a lot to them if I attended their next concert, and I agree to go. But then when the day comes, I forget and miss the concert. I will feel some guilt if I think, "Forgetting my friend's concert was bad." Shame refers to what we experience when we feel distress about our self—who we are as a person. For example, I will feel shame if I think, "I am a bad friend."

Guilt and shame are often considered to be feelings. They each certainly have an emotional component, which can be quite intense and which is almost always experienced as unpleasant. However, these are not purely emotions in the strict sense. To experience guilt or shame, we must also have thoughts that interpret the unpleasant feelings we are having as such. In the example, once I realize that I missed the concert, I will likely feel bad. I may experience a negative emotion like sadness for missing something that was important to my friend and to me. If I also have thoughts like, "I should have put it in my planner as soon I found out about it," or "I'm a terrible friend," I will experience the negative emotion as guilt and/or shame. In other words, guilt and shame are experiences of distressing emotions that largely arise from our interpretation of the situation and our actions. In a nutshell, guilt and shame each have a feeling component and a thinking component.

When guilt or shame shows up in a problematic way, as they tend to do in the context of trauma and adversity, you rarely see one without the other. They glom together and feed into and reinforce one another, resulting in a nasty cycle that becomes increasingly difficult to catch, stop, and escape. That is the type of guilt and shame I focus on in this book: the unhealthy guilt–shame cycle that wreaks havoc in our lives. Let us look at these emotions in a little more depth and how they can show up: the good, the bad, and the ugly.

THE GOOD: GUILT AND SHAME CAN BE HELPFUL!

Many people are surprised to hear that guilt and shame are not necessarily bad and, in fact, can be good for us. They feel bad to be sure. But having emotions helps us stay alive, even the ones—especially the ones—we typically describe as negative. When our brain perceives a danger, it triggers a survival response, which includes a strong emotional reaction that compels us to act in ways that help us survive. This happens when we experience a traumatic or adverse event. This could be an immediate danger or a potential threat to our life or physical or psychological well-being or that of someone we care about. Some examples are physical assault, sexual abuse, neglect, persecution, natural disasters, accidents, and combat. Many common adverse experiences cause extreme suffering even if their threat is less obvious or immediate. For example, being betrayed by someone or an institution that you trust or depend on and repeated or systemic discrimination experiences, even subtle ones (sometimes referred to as microaggressions), have been found to cause the same kind of suffering as what is more typically identified as trauma. When we experience such trauma or adversity, our hard-wired natural survival system kicks in and automatically activates survival responses.

Survival Response #1 to Trauma and Adversity: Fight–Flight–Freeze

The primary survival response is the *fight–flight–freeze* response. It's called this because fight, flight, and freeze are the only three behavioral options available to our automatic survival system. This is not something our logical thinking brain has much choice about. Our survival system is in charge, and it does a quick calculation to determine which of the three options is most likely to keep us alive. To determine the best course of action, our survival system considers the characteristics of the particular situation we're in, our resources (i.e., our abilities, knowledge, and training), and what may have helped us survive previous challenges.

The following are some examples of how this has played out with people I have worked with:

- When **Maxwell** became nervous that something dangerous was going to happen when he was on the crowded street in the Iraqi village, his survival mechanism compelled him to keep moving to get out of the potential danger's way (flight). Then, once the rocket-propelled grenade (RPG) exploded, his survival instinct was to return fire in the direction it came from (fight). The flight response made the most sense before the RPG exploded because Maxwell only had a sense that something could happen but no clear indication of what or where the danger might come from. He also had been trained to operate under the rules of engagement of that time, which included a prohibition against initiating any offensive or defensive combat action unless directly attacked. Once the explosion occurred, Maxwell was compelled to fight in the way he was trained to help keep civilians and his comrades safe, including shooting at the enemy.

- **Charmaine** froze during her multiple sexual assaults because she had little to no power relative to her abusers. Fighting against or fleeing from abusers can make them angry and more violent. Charmaine was much smaller and weaker than the man who abused her when she was a child, and she would not likely have been able to successfully fight him off or flee from him. She might have been bigger and stronger when she was assaulted as an adult, but she was still smaller and weaker than the assailant.
- **Duri** survived the earthquake by fleeing from the building that was crumbling around them.
- **Felipe** froze early on when being harassed and threatened. As he grew bigger and stronger and developed a decent social network, he was more likely to fight.
- **Saj** mostly froze whenever she was being emotionally or physically abused by her wife.

When you were confronted by your trauma or adversity, you also fought, fled, and/or froze, and that helped you survive. Once you were through the worst part, your survival system continued to operate for a while, albeit possibly less intensely, to make sure you remained safe. It tried to keep you on high alert to help you notice any further signs of danger or threat so you could avoid or quickly address any more bad things that may happen. This means that for a while, in all likelihood, you were not able to sleep soundly, you were on guard, your heart rate and breathing were faster than usual, and you were able to see, hear, smell, taste, and feel things you might not normally have been able to. During this time, shortly after experiencing a trauma or adversity, people often describe feeling like they are jumping out of their skin, restless, and suspicious—paranoid, even. Things keep going like this until the survival system gets the message that the threat of danger is over. Sometimes, though, the survival system doesn't get this message and stays on high alert long after it is needed. We'll come back to why that is. But first, let's turn to how guilt and shame are involved in the survival response.

Survival Response #2 to Trauma and Adversity: Guilt and Shame

Another way your survival system has tried to protect you in the face of threat is to compel you to learn everything you can from the situation in case there is any knowledge you might gain from it that could help you prevent it from happening again. When something bad happens, we feel bad, which initially feels like guilt and/or shame. This is good for our survival because it makes us want to figure out if anything we did (or didn't do) caused the adverse event. If there is something you did that in any way contributed to the adversity and you can figure out what that something is, that would mean you may have some power to prevent it from happening again or at least make things better more quickly. And that would be a good thing.

Guilt and shame are also beneficial to your survival because they are *prosocial* feelings. This means they compel us to behave in ways that help us stay socially connected, which is important because, as human beings, we are dependent on others for our survival. We have a better chance of staying alive when we are part of a group than when we are on our own. Therefore, we are more likely to survive if we act in ways that make it more likely we are accepted, supported, and protected by others. Feeling guilt and shame and the desire to avoid feeling guilt and shame compel us to act in these prosocial ways.

Let's consider my example about feeling some guilt about missing my friend's concert. Feeling guilt is aversive, which compels me to try to do things to avoid feeling it again. Therefore, I will want to take some time to figure out what I can do to not miss the next special event. For example, I might start putting things in my planner as soon as I learn about events, setting reminders on my phone a day ahead of events and just before, and/or asking another friend to remind me. I might even reduce the number of hours I work if that is getting in the way of my ability to think and plan ahead. You get the idea. Feeling guilt compels me to make changes in my behavior that will reduce the likelihood of me feeling guilt for not following through on plans in the future. And that will make it more likely that my relationship with my friend stays intact, that we continue to trust each other and know we can count on each other when needed. Having others who have my back increases my chances of survival.

Similarly, if I feel shame about missing my friend's concert, I will also be compelled to do something to reduce that feeling and maybe even more so. For many people, feeling shame is more aversive than feeling guilt, so the desire to not experience it can be even stronger. Because of this, the things we do to stop feeling shame tend to be bigger than what we do to stop feeling guilt, and our actions are usually more directly focused on making sure we are not rejected by others. In my missed concert example, feeling shame would compel me to apologize, offer to make up for it somehow, promise to be there for my friend the next time, and explain or even demonstrate the changes I have made to ensure that I will.

The more dependent we are on others (e.g., for shelter, food, safety, job security, money, sense of worth) and the greater the threat of disconnection we feel, the more intense and immediate our shame reaction is. Have you ever found that your posture and behavior change when you feel shame? You might have noticed that you hunch your shoulders, lower your head, avoid eye contact, or even turn or move your body away from others. You may try to be quiet and make yourself small or even invisible. You may not feel particularly good in this shame stance, but it can be quite adaptive. Adopting a shame stance doesn't feel good because it is a way to demonstrate to others that we are taking a one-down position. But in some situations, showing deference and that we are not threatening to others is the very thing that will help increase our chance of survival. This is particularly true when we are confronted by someone who has some power over us, like a parent or caregiver with a child or a boss with an employee or a member of a combat team. If a person I am dependent on is abusing me or threatening to reject me, my assuming a deferent, nonthreatening shame stance is more likely to help diffuse their aggression or threat than fighting or fleeing would, and I will therefore be more likely to be able to maintain attachment to them.

I know this sounds crazy. Why would I want to maintain an attachment to someone who is mistreating me? It's because my brain has done quick calculations and determined that, at this moment, that person's abuse of me, no matter how severe, is less threatening to my survival than losing what resources or protection they provide for me. And my survival brain doesn't care if that is what I want or think I need. Its only function is to make me do what I have to do to increase my chance of staying alive, and if that means maintaining an attachment to someone who is abusive, then so be it.

In summary, guilt and shame are good because they are *adaptive*. They play an important role in increasing our chances of survival by helping us maintain critical social relationships. For better or worse, human beings are more likely to survive if they have others available and willing to support, assist, and protect them. And guilt and shame can help us act in ways that keep people wanting to support, assist, and protect us.

THE BAD: NONADAPTIVE GUILT AND SHAME

Once the imminent danger has subsided, and we have given it a good think through and learned everything we can from the situation, we no longer need to feel or act on the guilt or shame, and these emotions dissipate on their own. Sometimes, though, we get stuck with guilt and shame long past their usefulness. This may be where you're at: stuck with nonadaptive guilt and shame, or NAGS for short. This is an appropriate acronym because it does feel like your brain is nagging at you. How and why do good guilt and shame become bad guilt and shame? It turns out this is more likely to happen in the context of trauma and adversity. I review some of the main reasons next.

Reason #1 We Get Stuck With NAGS: We Believe False Conclusions

We get stuck with NAGS if we believe the negative things that our guilt and shame tell us, regardless of what the facts might be, and we are more likely to do this when those feelings are strong. Have you ever noticed that it is difficult to think clearly, objectively, or rationally about anything when you are experiencing intense feelings? I definitely have. That happens partly because our emotions are an important part of our survival system, as we have already reviewed. When our survival brain perceives a threat, it sounds the alarm, which comes in the form of strong emotions (e.g., fear, guilt, and shame). The stronger our emotions are, the more likely we are ruled by them, which is useful for our survival. We are compelled to run away (flee) when experiencing strong fear. Anger helps us confront and fight. We feel obliged to ask for forgiveness if we feel guilt. We act in deference toward others if we feel shame. These behaviors, prompted by strong emotions, increase the chance that we will survive different scenarios.

Unfortunately, however, having strong emotions is not so great for coming to accurate conclusions. The more intense our feelings, the more we take them as facts. This means that the negative conclusions our guilt and shame tell us can too easily be taken at face value instead of as a side effect of emotions that prompt adaptive survival behaviors. The intensity of the feelings is seen as proof that we are guilty or have good reason to be ashamed.

Reason #2 We Get Stuck With NAGS: We Avoid

The second reason we get stuck with unhelpful guilt and shame is that we have a natural tendency to want to avoid emotions we find aversive. Recall that this can be adaptive because it urges us to behave in ways that increase our chance of survival by making us steer clear of whatever we think caused the unwanted emotions, including things we believe we have done to contribute to them. The problem is that human beings have created shortcuts to avoiding unpleasant things. In fact, we have discovered or invented seemingly unending ways that help distract ourselves from our thoughts and feelings—for example, scrolling through social media, shopping, engaging in risky behaviors like extreme sports or speeding, drinking alcohol, or taking other drugs, to name just a few. These activities can be quite effective in helping us avoid unwanted emotions like guilt and shame.

Unfortunately, their effectiveness is short-lived, so we have to keep engaging in one or another to keep avoiding our unwanted feelings. Engaging in these avoidance shortcuts interferes with us taking the steps that will be most adaptive to our survival in the long run, like letting our emotions prompt honest inquiry and corrective action if needed. When we don't let ourselves feel emotions of guilt or shame, we don't allow ourselves the chance to learn anything from the situation that might be helpful in the future, and we don't allow ourselves the chance to objectively evaluate what these emotions seem to be communicating. So, the guilt and shame end up sticking around longer than if we allowed ourselves to feel them and let them take their natural adaptive course. In other words, they become NAGS.

I want to be clear here. I am not suggesting that if you engage in avoidance behaviors you always do so purposefully. For sure, probably sometimes you do so. We all have times when we just want to escape, have down time, or even hole up in bed in a fetal position and block out the world. A lot of the time, however, we can avoid without purposely setting out to do so and without being aware that we wanted to avoid.

One powerful force that can make us engage in avoidance behaviors without necessarily intending to is social dependence. As I explained earlier in this chapter, when we are dependent on a person who is abusing us or threatening to reject us, such as a parent or abusive spouse, there are specific ways of dealing with that kind of situation to increase our survival odds that are different than when the perpetrator is a stranger who doesn't have any power over us. While it may be a good survival strategy to confront (fight) or withdraw from (flee) an assailant I am not dependent on, neither option may be the best course of action if, at that time, my survival depends more on my maintaining attachment with the assailant than eliminating the potential threat of their abuse.

Therefore, when attachment is important to maintain, our survival system will do whatever it can to turn off the confront (fight) and withdraw (flight) reactions. One of its main strategies is to interfere with our awareness or ability to understand that we are being mistreated or threatened by the person we are dependent on. It keeps us from being fully aware of the abuse so we can maintain attachment with them and increase our chance of survival. As already reviewed, we have an abundance of ways we can avoid our thoughts and feelings. One tactic often used to maintain attachment is to take on the guilt and shame. Recall the shame stance I explained earlier, which serves us well in this kind of scenario. The problem arises when we have to maintain that for some time because our mind usually helps us by making up a story that often involves taking on misplaced guilt and shame, as the following case example illustrates.

For **Charmaine** to survive as a kid, she had to maintain an attachment with her parents' best friends, who took care of her during several weeks of her summer breaks. The fact that she was so young and had no knowledge of sex helped her stay unaware of the abuse. She had no language for what her abusive caregiver was doing to her or how it made her feel or why. Her limited experiences and knowledge made it easy for her mind to make up stories that would make the fight or flight responses less likely to be activated. Her mind convinced her that it must be normal, that she owed it to her caregiver to please him because he was doing her a favor by babysitting her, that she had no right to want or ask for anything different (and even just thinking that she did would mean she was a selfish brat), that she must have asked for it—that she must have given him a signal that she wanted him to do what he did to her or that there was just something wrong with her that gave off that impression. Believing these stories allowed her to maintain attachment.

Yes, imposing guilt and shame on herself created all sorts of other problems, not the least of which was feeling bad about herself. But Charmaine did avoid the greater distress and danger she would have experienced had she engaged in any behavior that might have strained her attachment to her perpetrator.

Reason #3 We Get Stuck With NAGS:
We Create a Self-Reinforcing Cycle

It is not surprising that we human beings invest a lot of time and effort in activities that help us avoid unwanted experiences. First, our automatic survival mechanism will help us avoid anything it perceives as dangerous. But the second contributor to avoidance, and the one that has compelled us to invent one and a half million avoidance shortcuts, is that it is self-reinforcing. Anything we do that has a desired or pleasant outcome (in this case, relief from danger or distress) is rewarding, and anything that is rewarding we are more likely to want to do again. Unfortunately, the reward from avoidance is short-lived, and we have to engage in it more and more or find different ways to get the same relieving effect. Meanwhile, unchecked misplaced guilt and shame just keep getting stronger, and we believe them more, so we want to avoid them more, and before we know it, we're stuck in a self-reinforcing NAGS cycle.

Figure 1.1 illustrates that cycle. When something bad happens, we feel bad. We feel intense negative emotions, including guilt and shame (indicated by the top circle in the graphic). If we come to conclusions that are not entirely accurate or helpful because they are based on feelings more than facts (right circle), we continue to feel bad and probably even worse (bottom circle), so we try different things to try to avoid feeling bad (left circle). But we can only avoid so much before the shame and guilt creep up again (top circle), and we are not able to objectively think about what happened and so continue to believe the inaccurate and unhelpful conclusions (right circle), and so on. Thus, NAGS not only stick around but also get bigger and stronger.

NAGS get worse, which makes it less likely we can think clearly and objectively and more likely that we will continue to be convinced by our inaccurate and unhelpful conclusions, so we feel worse and avoid more, and on and on it goes. Does this sound familiar to you

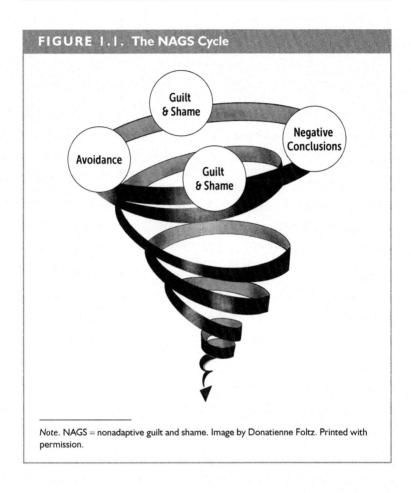

FIGURE 1.1. The NAGS Cycle

Note. NAGS = nonadaptive guilt and shame. Image by Donatienne Foltz. Printed with permission.

at all? When you're stuck in this NAGS cycle, you're miserable. The bad feelings just get worse. Even if you become really good at avoiding them, they will still rear their ugly heads, often when you least expect or want them to.

Unfortunately, that's not the worst of it. Being stuck in the NAGS cycle also results in a lot of other unwanted side effects, many of which are downright destructive. That's when guilt and shame turn ugly.

THE UGLY: THE DESTRUCTIVE SIDE EFFECTS
OF THE NAGS CYCLE

If you are stuck in a NAGS cycle, you probably are experiencing any number of its destructive side effects like anxiety, depression, chronic pain, irritability, being haunted by past adversities in your sleep or waking thoughts and reactions, relationship problems, difficulty concentrating or remembering important things, overusing alcohol or drugs, or engaging in other risky activities. Or maybe you have been experiencing other problems. Here are what NAGS side effects looked like in some of the people I worked with.

When he returned from Iraq, **Maxwell** was diagnosed with posttraumatic stress disorder. His memories of the RPG explosion kept popping into his head in vivid flashes of sights, sounds, and smells. He also frequently had scary nightmares of the blast, as well as other life-threatening situations. He constantly felt on edge and had difficulty completing even the simplest tasks, which was a new experience for him—he was used to being the most competent guy in the room. Maxwell found it hard to be around people whose company he used to enjoy. He no longer felt like he belonged. He lost trust in others and in his own judgment. His relationship with his partner deteriorated, and they separated.

Over the past 35 years since her last sexual assault, **Charmaine** smoked cigarettes and drank two to four screwdrivers per day. She described getting married because she felt she needed a husband to keep her safe. Charmaine remarked that she had never felt love for her husband nor ever felt close to anyone, including her adult son. She felt equally dispassionate about her job and pretty much everything else and reported not really having any joy in her life. Charmaine noticed she had gotten increasingly angry over time, to the point that she was getting aggressive toward others. She also experienced frequent migraines and chronic gastrointestinal problems.

Before the earthquake, **Duri** would have described themself as happy-go-lucky, being able to make friends with anyone, and enjoying their work and many hobbies. Following the earthquake, however, they were constantly on edge, on guard, and no longer able to enjoy the moment (something they were good at before). Duri often appeared tense, shoulders almost touching their ears, and exhibiting stiff, jerky movements or fidgeting. They were easily startled, jumping up and gasping at the slightest sounds coming from outside or adjacent offices.

Felipe came to therapy after he noticed himself getting increasingly angry and aggressive. He reported giving up on relationships because he couldn't count on others. He said people always ended up betraying or abandoning him. He had lost several jobs over a short time due to interpersonal issues and angry outbursts. He said cannabis was the only thing that helped him keep his temper.

When she first started therapy, **Saj** showed up unkempt, dressed in worn-out, oversized clothing. She moved slowly and deliberately and spoke quietly. It was like pulling teeth to get any information from her. She answered my questions with one or two words and made little eye contact. She lived with her son, from whom she felt increasingly disconnected. She had difficulty applying for and obtaining employment and did not socialize. Saj described herself as a "doormat," unable to ask for what she wants, always trying to please others, and constantly apologizing for things she knows are not her fault.

Perhaps you recognize yourself in one or more of these stories. Like them, you are stuck in a self-reinforcing guilt and shame loop, and you are experiencing some of its problematic side effects. You may be finding that your life has become small compared to what it used to be or what you once thought it might have been. Maybe you, too, are feeling unhappy and that you have little or no power to make things better. You don't feel like you hold the reins but instead are living your life as if you are sitting on a wagon that is being pulled by wild horses who have their own agendas that have nothing to do with what you want or need.

That's because being stuck in a NAGS cycle means you are no longer calling all the shots. Your survival system is stuck in overdrive and is, therefore, holding the reins most of the time, and you're working with a map that is not accurate. It's hard for anyone to reach their desired destination when they have a bad map. And a map based on NAGS is rife with wrong turns that are not in our best interest and end up making us feel more guilt and shame. For example, if I believe that I have done something bad and, therefore, that I am bad and will inevitably do bad things, I will not bother listening to my conscience trying to talk me out of doing something that goes against my values. If I believe I am deserving of bad things, I will not bother being assertive or setting boundaries, which will only make it easier for others to take advantage of me.

The map we have when we're stuck in a NAGS cycle is also filled with avoidance paths. Besides keeping us stuck in a spiral of ever-escalating NAGS, avoidance can cause other problems. First, it's not selective and generalizes to other areas we might not want to avoid, like things that are important to us. Have you noticed that you have difficulty meeting deadlines, procrastinate more than you would like, don't complete things you have started, have a list of to-dos that is piling up, or don't follow through with things you promised yourself or others you would do? If you have noticed any of these things, you might be dealing with this kind of overgeneralized avoidance. Here is what it looked like for one of my clients.

Whenever **Saj** had downtime, her brain was in the habit of rehearsing old negative refrains about herself and her life. She, therefore, was usually engaged in some distracting activity. Her go-tos were watching funny animal videos, eating sweets, drinking wine, and gossiping with her coworkers. She also always had the television on, even throughout the night, so she was never in silence. She found that doing these things made her feel better than sitting alone with her thoughts. However, she also often found that she distracted herself so much that before she knew it, many hours had passed, and she had forgotten to do something important. Sometimes, it was way past dinnertime, and she had not made dinner for herself or her son. Sometimes, she missed meetings she had planned with a friend or didn't finish something she was supposed to have ready for work the next day. This added to her guilt and shame as her mind played the old familiar refrain: "See? There is something wrong with me. I can't be trusted or depended on. I am a bad mother. I am a terrible person."

The other problem with avoidance is that some of the most common strategies we use are unhealthy or downright harmful or go against our values. These include consuming too much alcohol or too many drugs, sleeping too much or not enough, engaging in risky behaviors like driving too fast or having lots of unprotected sex with different partners, eating too much or too little, overexercising, gambling, self-stimulating to such an extent that it causes physical harm, intentionally self-harming, and overworking. Have you found yourself increasingly engaging in behaviors that you know are detrimental to your physical or mental health? If so, know that you're not alone. It is part of the human tendency to prioritize immediate feel-good sensations (e.g., avoiding distress right now) over any less immediate outcome (e.g., feeling better in the long run). And when we are stuck in a NAGS cycle, this tendency is heightened. This is how it played out for another client.

Duri wasn't aware of it for over a decade, but when they started paying attention to their thoughts, feelings, and behaviors, they realized that they were engaging in harmful avoidance behaviors. Duri occasionally drank alcohol and took cannabis recreationally before the earthquake. But they did not do so frequently, and it never interfered with their work or other activities. After the earthquake, though, Duri found that partaking in alcohol or cannabis provided a much-welcomed reprieve from the anxiety and panic that seemed to be becoming constant companions, as well as the insomnia. Without noticing, Duri quickly started using one or both of these substances daily. Initially, this was in the evening, "just so I can fall asleep." Then, Duri began drinking earlier and earlier in the day. First, it was a glass of wine with dinner, then it became two. A little later, the drinking started earlier, with a beer when they got home from work. Then Duri started taking cannabis earlier too. It got to the point that they often took an edible before work in the morning because they felt they were too anxious to function well at work.

On reflection, Duri was able to see the paradox of the things they were doing to reduce their anxiety and insomnia actually making them worse (which caused them to increase their intake to get the desired effects). Duri also experienced increasing difficulty remembering things and focusing. It took them much longer to get tasks done at work than it used to. Their regular alcohol and cannabis use not only contributed to these psychological concerns but also to physical health problems. They were often sick and had to take time off work. They found it more difficult to do physical activities because they experienced pain and shortness of breath. They also ate more, and the foods they ate tended to be processed, which resulted in weight gain and related pain and mobility issues. Their last medical exam revealed signs of early liver damage and high blood pressure.

CONCLUSION

Because you are reading this book and you've gotten to this point, I will assume you are stuck in an ugly NAGS cycle. You have lost your grip on the reins of your life. Instead of choosing how you respond to any given situation, you often react in what feels like an automatic way that is largely out of your hands and not in your best interest or in line with your values. Most people find a life in which they are not holding the reins to be quite unsettling and not meaningful or fulfilling at best, and to induce a sense of helplessness and hopelessness at worst. Do you find yourself somewhere on this continuum? If so, that would not be surprising. Being stuck in the NAGS cycle does that.

What I want to make clear at this point is that you are not helpless, and there is hope. Your guilt and shame were activated by your safety system to help you survive, and your brain did the best it could to try to make sense of these feelings, given the information it had and the context you were in. Ultimately, though, you are smarter than your survival brain, and it is within you to learn to have a different relationship with it so you can use it as the superpower it is but not let it dictate your whole life. You can retake the reins of your life. You can regain your agency, make choices that are in your best interest, and have a life that feels meaningful to you. This book will lead you through the steps to get yourself out of the NAGS cycle and have guilt and shame work adaptively for you instead of against you.

CHAPTER 2

WHAT NAGS YOU?

Now that you understand what guilt and shame are and how they can cause you problems, get ready to start the transformation process so they can serve you well instead. Because of how our minds work during trauma and adversity, while focused on survival in the moment, they can initially produce many thoughts that are not 100% accurate. Let's see if everything your mind has been telling you is true. If not, let's figure out what else you could be telling yourself that is more accurate and, therefore, more helpful moving forward. If your mind has been telling you some things that are true, there are probably lots of things you could be doing with that truth that are more helpful than what you have been doing (e.g., avoiding or overcompensating, which just serve to keep you stuck in the non-adaptive guilt and shame [NAGS] cycle). So, either way, engaging in this process is a win–win.

We will start by making a list of all the guilt and shame conclusions you may have come to. Our avoidance often does a good job of keeping NAGS thoughts hidden from us, and it is helpful to use different strategies to uncover them. As you uncover NAGS thoughts, you may experience a surge of strong emotions, including guilt and shame. This is quite normal and a good sign. So don't hesitate to confront your unhealthy thoughts even if your survival brain starts raising the alarm and you have urges to avoid. You can thank it for doing what it thinks it needs to do to help keep you alive. But you can also remind it and yourself that your feelings are loud because the avoidance has intensified them. Remind yourself that you are currently safe and that thinking about things that happened in the past doesn't mean they are happening again right now. Remind yourself that instead of getting weighed down by your thoughts and feelings, you can simply notice them and write them all down.

WRITING EXERCISE: IDENTIFY YOUR NAGS THOUGHTS

Start by thinking about the trauma or adverse event about which you feel the most distressing amounts of guilt and shame. Focus on one event or situation at a time. You can work through others in turn as needed later. You will benefit most by starting with the situation related to the most guilt and shame. And you may find that the positive effects generalize to any other guilt- or shame-inducing situation. So, spend some time thinking about the trauma or adverse event. Then write about it in Worksheet 2.1. Write down everything you can recall about the series of events and your thoughts, feelings, and behaviors leading up to, during, and immediately following the adverse event. If you would like to download and save digital copies or print hard copies of this or any of the other worksheets, you can do so from https://www.apa.org/pubs/books/transform-your-guilt-shame (see the Resources tab).

As you think, notice when guilt and shame feelings pop up and what they are about. In Worksheet 2.2, write down any thoughts that might make you feel guilt or shame. For example,

- Do you think you did anything wrong? If so, what?
- Do you think you should have done something differently? If so, what?

- Do you think you should have reacted differently? If so, how?
- Do you think you did something to cause the adverse event to happen? If so, what?
- Do you think you could or should have prevented what happened? If so, how?
- Do you think you should have known better? If so, why?
- Do you think you should have felt differently? If so, how should you have felt? Why?
- Do you think you should have thought differently? If so, how should you have thought and why?
- Do you have other "should" or "shouldn't" thoughts about the situation?
- Do you think you are a bad person or there is something wrong with you?
- Do you think you deserved what happened? Or do you think you deserve bad things to happen or don't deserve good things to happen?

Take your time with this. Write down as many of these thoughts as possible, even if you think some are saying the same thing. Don't edit yourself.

Once you have written your answers to the questions from the bulleted list into Worksheet 2.2, look over some of the most common guilt and shame thoughts I come across as a therapist (discussed in the case examples below) and see if there are any that resonate with you that you have not identified yet. Of course, your circumstances were not identical to those of any of these folks, so your conclusions may have different details. But you may find some that have the same gist. Write these down in Worksheet 2.2 if they apply to you.

Maxwell, who witnessed the wounding or death of several fellow service members and civilians from the rocket-propelled

WORKSHEET 2.1. Play-by-Play of the Trauma or Adverse Event

Write about the trauma or adverse event. Write down everything you can recall about the series of events and your thoughts, feelings, and behaviors leading up to, during, and immediately following the adverse event.

WORKSHEET 2.2. Guilt and Shame Thoughts

Write down all thoughts that come up that make you feel guilt or shame when you think about the trauma or adversity you experienced. You will need to return to this worksheet a few times, so you might want to place a bookmark here or fold over the corner of this page so that you can quickly find it.

grenade blast, identified the following beliefs that led him to feel guilt and shame:

- I should have pushed my commanding officer more to take action when I sensed that something was unsafe.
- I should have disregarded my commands, taken action, and looked for and offensively addressed the source of the danger I sensed.
- I should have taken evasive action.
- I should have urged others to take evasive action.
- I should have died instead of X, who was a much better person.
- I should not be alive when others are dead.

Charmaine identified the following guilt and shame thoughts about the sexual abuse by her dad's best friend:

- I should have stopped him and said no.
- I should have run away.
- I should have told my parents, someone, anyone.
- There was part of me that enjoyed the attention, so I must have somehow asked for it or put out signals that I wanted it.
- I felt some physical pleasure, so I must be bad.
- I must have deserved it.

Charmaine had many of these same thoughts about the sexual assault she experienced as a young adult, in addition to the following:

- I should have known he was no good, that he was going to assault me.
- I shouldn't have gone outside the bar with the guy.
- I should have fought him off.

Saj, who experienced domestic violence for many years, came to believe the following:

- I should have known she had the potential to be violent.
- I shouldn't have stayed in the relationship or married her or had a child.
- I should have known it was going to continue or get worse.
- I should have left the first time she yelled at me, called me names, and definitely after the first time she hit me.
- I should have fought back.
- I should have told someone or reported it.
- I should have prevented our child from being exposed to the violence.

Duri's reactions during the earthquake made them think:

- I shouldn't have gone there.
- I should have been better prepared.
- I shouldn't have been so scared.
- I am bad for not having stayed and helped others.
- I don't deserve to have lived when others died.

Felipe felt guilt and shame about the harassment he experienced because of the following thoughts:

- I should have tried harder to fit in.
- There must be something wrong with me; I have less worth than others.
- I should have done something to stop it, fought back sooner, told someone, or asked for help.
- I shouldn't have antagonized them.

If any of these sound like thoughts you have about your situation, add them to your list on Worksheet 2.2.

FIVE TYPES OF NAGS THOUGHTS

Now that you have collected your guilt and shame thoughts, the next step is to sort them. There are five main types of conclusions that we can come to when we have initial feelings of guilt and shame and that we keep reinforcing when we are stuck in a NAGS cycle. These five types of conclusions are (a) foreseeability and preventability, (b) insufficient justification, (c) responsibility, (d) wrongdoing, and (e) violated values. You might imagine separating your thoughts into five piles, like you might sort your laundry according to how the items need to be washed and dried (see Figure 2.1). Over the next five chapters, we will sort your thoughts into these five piles and deal with one pile at a time because we sometimes need to apply different strategies to effectively deal with each pile, just as different types of clothing need different wash and dry settings.

For each category, I'll help you identify thoughts you might have that belong to that pile. Then, I'll describe the strategies you can take to evaluate your thoughts so you can allow yourself to come to more helpful and accurate conclusions. I will provide examples of how some of my clients have worked through these steps and how they have benefited from doing so. You will then put what you have learned into practice using the worksheets in this book.

You can work at your own pace. You can choose to tackle one pile now and others on different days. You can process all the piles in one sitting. You can also read through the entire book first if you're one of those people who likes to see the big picture before you start. Just be aware that reading alone will not likely help you with your guilt and shame. So don't let your mind fool you into thinking you are doing the work if you are just reading each section and not doing

---

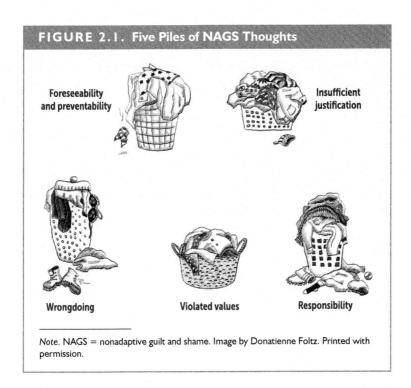

FIGURE 2.1. Five Piles of NAGS Thoughts

Foreseeability and preventability

Insufficient justification

Wrongdoing

Violated values

Responsibility

Note. NAGS = nonadaptive guilt and shame. Image by Donatienne Foltz. Printed with permission.

the exercises. Be sure to come back to each chapter and complete the exercises if you want to benefit from them.

As you would do if you were going through trauma informed guilt reduction therapy (commonly referred to as TrIGR) with a therapist, you are encouraged to work through each strategy presented in the following chapters one at a time, carefully and thoughtfully considering each question before moving on to the next. You should also be aware that folks often greatly benefit from working through the steps in this book more than once for some thoughts. Remember that your safety system thought it had to convince you of some things to keep you alive. And you may have been rehearsing and rewarding some thoughts for so long that they have become strong habits. They can feel like they are engraved in stone. So, your mind won't let go of these beliefs easily. I like to call these *sticky thoughts*. They are much like a stubborn stain that you have to wash more than once and you may need to let soak for a while before you remove it. With time and practice, you can break free from the cycle of unhealthy guilt and shame.

CONCLUSION

Feeling guilt and shame may have helped you survive trauma or adversity. But how your mind interpreted these emotions was not necessarily accurate. And these inaccurate conclusions have stuck with you even though they are no longer serving you. Now, though, you can reevaluate your interpretations and come to more accurate and helpful conclusions. That is what you will learn to do in the next chapters.

But if you stop here for today, thank yourself and take some time to reward yourself.

CHAPTER 3

CHALLENGE YOUR FORESEEABILITY AND PREVENTABILITY THOUGHTS

The first pile of nonadaptive guilt and shame (NAGS) thoughts we will tackle has to do with the belief that an adverse experience was foreseeable—that we predicted it and could see it coming—and, therefore, preventable and that because we did not prevent it, it is our fault that it happened. To what extent do you believe this? Look at the list of thoughts you wrote down in Worksheet 2.2. Do you have any thoughts that sound like any of the following?

- I should have known better.
- I should have listened to my intuition, noticed the red flags, or heeded the warnings.
- I should have seen it coming.

If yes, you are telling yourself what happened was foreseeable, you could and should have seen it coming, and therefore, you could and should have prevented it. In Worksheet 2.2, write "FP" next to any foreseeability and preventability thoughts.

Keep in mind that many thoughts can belong to more than one pile, so don't worry about whether a particular thought could also belong in one of the other piles. Put FP next to any thought you think might have some conclusions about whether you could or should have foreseen what was going to happen and should have done something to prevent or make the situation better. Also, as you continue to work through the book, you may start noticing you have more guilt and shame thoughts than you initially listed on Worksheet 2.2. That is normal and a good thing. Just keep adding them to your Worksheet 2.2. The more guilt and shame conclusions you expose, the more opportunity you have for challenging them and breaking free of the NAGS cycle.

That something was foreseeable and preventable is one of the most common conclusions we come to when we experience an adverse event. This is probably due to two fundamental human characteristics. First, we like to have a sense of control over things. Believing we could have prevented something helps us feel like we can prevent it from happening in the future. Second, we are susceptible to *hindsight bias*. That is, what we now know biases what we think we knew in the past.

UNDERSTAND THE ROLE OF HINDSIGHT BIAS

Once we know something happened, it is difficult for us to remember that we did not know what was going to happen before it happened. Hindsight bias, therefore, occurs when we believe we knew something in the past that we did not actually know until much later. For some reason probably related to our desire to have a sense of control over our destiny, it seems to be especially common for traumatic or adverse events.

So, the first step in evaluating whether you are correct in your thinking that something was foreseeable and, therefore, preventable is to notice and challenge any hindsight bias that might be at play. You can do this by taking some time to remember the adverse event and recall all the information you had at the time, as well as all the information you did not have at the time but obtained later. Here is how this played out for a couple of my clients.

CASE EXAMPLES OF HINDSIGHT BIAS

After the rocket-propelled grenade exploded, **Maxwell** became convinced that he had known something bad was going to happen before it did. Whenever he described what was going on before the explosion, he focused on remembering the thoughts and feelings that supported his belief that he foresaw the danger. He easily recalled feeling fear and a sense of trepidation and wanting to take some action to protect himself and others. This is part of what contributes to hindsight bias: We hyperfocus on things that are in line with our beliefs and minimize or ignore details that are not. When I asked Maxwell to recount the entire event from start to finish, only telling me what he definitely knew at the time and not what he knows now, he remembered other important pieces of information. Maxwell did indeed recall feeling nervous and worried that something bad would happen, but he also recalled that he did not know exactly what was going to happen or even that something would definitely happen. Moreover, he was reminded that he usually felt this way while deployed and most of the time, nothing bad happened despite him feeling this way. In addition, Maxwell remembered having checked in with his commanding officer who decided no action should be taken according to the data their team had collected. And he further recalled that he trusted his commanding officer and his team, that they were well trained to surveil and assess threat levels everywhere they went, and that they all stayed vigilant and reacted appropriately.

Saj, who believed she should have left her abusive partner sooner, also found that some of her conclusions were influenced by hindsight bias. Like Maxwell, Saj was adamant about having seen the red flags and blamed herself for ignoring them, subjecting herself to more violence and exposing her child to it. She, too, remembered these less as potential signs and more as clear fortune-telling that abuse was coming and it would get worse over time. When I asked her to walk me through the history of her relationship and instances of abuse, Saj recalled that she was shocked when her partner first hit her—she had not seen it coming. She said she did see some red flags: Her partner yelled at her when she was upset and sometimes threw, hit, or broke inanimate objects. But she also saw flags of other colors (e.g., white and green): Her partner always calmed herself down and apologized after she expressed anger in these ways, and she could be sweet and thoughtful at other times. Saj also remembered that she herself would yell and slam doors when she was upset, and it didn't mean she had any intention of hurting her partner. After reflecting on this a bit, Saj acknowledged she did not foresee that her partner was going to start physically abusing her after all.

However, she continued to blame herself for not leaving once her partner started being physically abusive toward her. She had convinced herself that once her partner shoved and slapped her in the middle of an argument the first time, she knew for sure her partner would continue to be abusive. She attempted to continue to challenge her hindsight bias and to remember what she did and did not know at the time, but this was only helpful to a limited extent. She continued to be certain that she must have known being hit this first time was a clear sign her partner would continue to be abusive and things would get worse. So, I turned to the next strategy. I asked her what my colleagues and I call the *million-dollar question*: "If you knew what was going to happen next, would you have done what you did, or would you have made different choices?" Like most people who respond to this question, Saj immediately gave me an emphatic "No! Of course not." She followed this response with something to the effect of, "I would have packed my bags and left as soon as I had the chance."

No sooner had the words come out of her mouth than she realized this was proof that she had not known for sure what the future held. If she had, she would have made different choices and taken different actions. She did not know for sure that her partner would continue to be abusive. In fact, she recalled having been in shock and not knowing what to think. She remembered wondering and worrying if it would happen again. But she also was thinking many other things, such as this was surely a one-off occurrence resulting from a combination of factors that were present at the time (e.g., her partner was under a great deal of stress at work, she just lost one of her best friends, they had just had a difficult parent–teacher meeting because their child was not doing well in a couple of classes). Saj recalled even believing she was to blame for making her partner angry during their argument because she called her names. She believed she should have been more considerate of the stress her partner was under and not been so mean.

Saj also had memories of her partner apologizing and attempting to change her behavior after she had been hurtful. Therefore, of course, Saj didn't pack her bags and leave. She still had reason to feel hopeful for the future of the relationship. She didn't know the abuse would continue or get worse. Moreover, because she blamed herself for the abuse, Saj fooled herself into thinking she had control over it and if she was more careful about when to bring up a disagreement or what she said, she could prevent it from happening again. This kind of thinking falls into the next couple of piles of thoughts, which we will address in the following chapters.

WRITING EXERCISE: NOTICE AND CHALLENGE YOUR HINDSIGHT BIAS

Challenge any conclusions of guilt and shame you have come to because you have convinced yourself that you knew what was going to happen and that you are, therefore, at fault because you didn't prevent it from happening. Start by taking some time to remember the details of the situation and all the information you had at the time. It can help to review what you wrote in Worksheet 2.1. Now, see if you can catch any hindsight bias (what you know now that you didn't know then), and take that out of the story you have been telling yourself. Literally, cross it out if you wrote it down in Worksheet 2.1. And don't keep repeating it to yourself.

In Worksheet 3.1, write down everything you didn't know when you made the decisions or took the actions you did. For example, you might write something such as the following:

> I wish I had known _____, but I didn't.
> There was no way for me to know for sure what was going to happen. I, therefore, could not have prevented it.

Next, ask yourself the million-dollar question: If you knew exactly what was going to happen, would you have done what you did, or would you have made different choices? If you answered that you would have done something different, you just proved to yourself that you didn't know for sure what was going to happen, and therefore, you couldn't have prevented it. Write this down in Worksheet 3.1, too.

If you answered that you would have done the same thing(s) and you feel guilt and shame about it, then ask yourself why. Are you telling yourself you are bad, or there is something wrong with you for wanting what happened to have taken place? If these conclusions are not already on your Worksheet 2.2, write them down there. The strategies in the subsequent chapters will help you evaluate those kinds of conclusions to see if they are 100% true or if there are other things you could be telling yourself that are more accurate and helpful.

If you don't think foreseeability and preventability conclusions apply to you regarding a trauma or adverse event you experienced, you can still practice following the steps to challenge your

WORKSHEET 3.1. New, More Accurate, and Helpful Thoughts

Each time you check and challenge one of your guilt and shame thoughts, write your new, more helpful conclusions that are based on the facts on this worksheet. This is where you will collect all your new, more accurate conclusions that you will come to by completing the exercises in the book. You could place a bookmark here or fold over the corner of this page so you can quickly find it and return to it. If you end up printing extra copies of it (which you can do from https://www.apa.org/pubs/books/transform-your-guilt-shame; see the Resources tab), you can tuck them in here to keep all your new, more accurate, and helpful thoughts in one place.

conclusions about other situations they might apply to. This will build up your skills and could help prevent problematic guilt and shame from latching on in the future.

CONCLUSION

Now that you have conducted the foreseeability and preventability analysis, you can tackle the next pile of thoughts. Don't worry if you still believe some of your old conclusions to some extent. Remember that it can take a while for our minds to open up to other ways of thinking, especially when they are convinced they have to stick to old beliefs to stay alive or have had a long time to rehearse and reinforce them. You can always return to this chapter to reread it and go through the exercises again. It can also be particularly helpful to reread all the challenging responses and reminders you wrote in Worksheet 3.1. So, take some time to review what you have written in this worksheet every day or so until the new, more accurate conclusions start to feel more familiar than your old thoughts. Changing an old way of thinking into a new way of thinking is just like replacing an old habit with a new one. Practice is key.

CHAPTER 4

CHALLENGE YOUR INSUFFICIENT JUSTIFICATION THOUGHTS

We can also feel guilt and shame when we believe we made the wrong decision about what to do in a situation with a bad outcome. We may think we had better options and no good reason for choosing the option we did. Have you been thinking this? Do you have thoughts that sound like the following?

- I was not justified in what I did.
- I shouldn't have done what I did.
- Instead of _____ (i.e., what you did), I should have _____.
- There was no good reason for what I did.
- I didn't have a good reason for doing what I did.
- There was a better option that I should have chosen.
- I can't trust my own judgment.

These are the kinds of thoughts that make up the second pile: insufficient justification. Go back to Worksheet 2.2 and add any of these thoughts that resonate with you if you don't already have them listed, and mark these and any other thoughts that fall into this pile by putting "IJ" next to them. Remember that thoughts can belong to more than one pile, so don't worry if you already marked a thought as belonging to the foreseeability and preventability pile. Also, as always, keep adding to Worksheet 2.2 any other guilt or shame thoughts you identify having as you keep reading and working through the book.

REASONS FOR INSUFFICIENT JUSTIFICATION CONCLUSIONS

It is easy to conclude that you should have acted differently when the outcome was bad (as in the case of trauma or adversity). The following line of thinking is all too common: "Something bad happened, so I must have made the wrong decision, right? There must have been something I should have done that would have made things better." When we come to this type of conclusion, though, we forget that there are rarely any good options when it comes to adverse events. It's like being stuck between a rock and a hard place: The best choice is the lesser of two evils. Our best option is the one that has the least bad possible outcomes compared with all the other options available to us at the time.

Another reason it's easy to believe what we did was not justified is the common human tendency of falling prey to hindsight bias, introduced in Chapter 3. It's easy to think of other things we could have and should have done after the fact. When not under threat, we have the luxury of time and access to the problem-solving part of our brains without interference from the survival part. Hindsight bias can lead us to believe that options we come up with after the fact were available to us at the time when, in actuality, they were not. Options are only available if we think of them.

Consider this simple example of what goes into making a choice. Let's say I am your friend, and I ask for your advice about selecting between two job offers: A promotion with my current employer that comes with a raise and another job at a different company that comes with an even bigger raise. You help me weigh the pros and cons of both options, and we agree that taking the promotion is the better option for me. So, I accept the promotion. But then, 2 weeks later, I call you up all upset, saying we made the wrong decision and I should have waited and applied to another position that just opened up. Would that be a fair conclusion? Of course not. It was not an available option at the time I had to make the decision. It would not be fair or rational to accuse you or me of having made the wrong decision. Yet we do this often. We judge ourselves for not making a choice that wasn't available to us at the time, especially when the outcome was bad.

It would also be unfair to make myself feel guilty for not choosing an option I did not have the ability or resources to act on. For example, what if, in addition to the two job options I had, I was also offered a job in Italy? If I didn't have a European Union passport or the resources needed to obtain a working visa, it wouldn't make sense even to consider that option or blame myself after the fact for not choosing it. Options are only available if we think of them and have the resources and ability to act on them when we do think of them.

Finally, we can also develop a fantasy about how much better the outcome would have been had we done something else, and this fantasizing can lead us to negatively judge what we did. Returning to the example about choosing between jobs, let's say a month into my promotion, I am unhappy with it because I am working many more hours than I used to, and one of the people on my team constantly complains. I call to tell you we made a mistake because I wouldn't have had those problems had I taken the other job. How do you think you would react? I bet you would remind me I have no way of knowing that. You might tell me it's common to have to work with at least one person we find difficult. You would probably also remind me it's normal to work more hours than usual when starting a new job, and I probably would have to work even more hours if I started a position at an entirely new company because I would have much more to learn. Again, it wouldn't be fair to judge a decision

I made based on a fantasy about what I think the outcome would have been if I had decided on a different course of action. But this is also something we do a lot.

Do you have any thoughts that belong in this pile? Do you have any thoughts related to decisions you made that you think were not justifiable? What do you think you should have done instead? Are you sure that was an option you had at the time? Did you think of it? Did you have the information and resources to act on it? What do you think would have happened if you did act on it? Do you know for sure what would have happened? To help you answer these questions, it can be helpful to conduct a systematic analysis of all the options you had at the time. I next describe what this justification analysis looked like for a couple of my clients, and then we can work on yours.

CASE EXAMPLES OF JUSTIFICATION ANALYSIS: EVALUATING OPTIONS

Charmaine initially expressed guilt and shame about being assaulted outside the bar because she thought she shouldn't have been flirting with the man, and she especially shouldn't have gone outside with him. She also convinced herself that she should have fought him off. Charmaine successfully challenged the first thought by conducting a foreseeability and preventability analysis. She was able to recall that she did not suspect any ill intent on his part, nor did she have any reason to. Their conversations and his actions up to that point led her to believe he was genuinely interested in getting to know her, and she felt the same about him. She even recalled him showing some signs of being respectful and protective, putting himself between her and a group of people who were getting drunk and stumbling around, for instance. She acknowledged that she did not and could not have foreseen that he was going to assault her.

But she still blamed herself for doing nothing to stop it once he started abusing her. She had convinced herself that because she "passively took it," she must have wanted it, which meant she was bad and deserved to be treated badly. Because of the childhood abuse by her summer babysitter, Charmaine already had a preconceived notion that she was bad, so she was quick to jump to the conclusion that she made bad choices. This was especially easy for her when bad things happened. Therefore, she made assumptions such as, "I was assaulted, so I must have made a bad move." It was clear that Charmaine had rehearsed this conclusion without ever considering whether she had better options at the time. To help her do this, I invited her again to imagine herself back in the moment and to check any hindsight bias at the door. I asked her to write down all the options she had at the time. She identified the following, starting with what she remembered doing (doing nothing or "taking it"):

- **Option A:** Do nothing.
- **Option B:** Fight back.
- **Option C:** Yell for help.
- **Option D:** Get away.
- **Option E:** Call 911.

Next, I asked her to list the pros and cons she considered or could imagine considering at the time for each option. I asked her to think about what she knew then and what she thought might happen if she had chosen each option. Table 4.1 shows what she initially came up with.

I then asked her to review the pros and cons of each option. Doing this helped her realize she had no good option—each one left her with the likely outcome of being assaulted, and several had the possibility of making things worse. When she thought about it, Charmaine also noticed that a few options may have been

TABLE 4.1. Charmaine's Justification Analysis

	Options	Pros	Cons
A	Do nothing	May get less hurt if I don't resist or confront him, over with faster	Get assaulted, hurt
B	Fight back	May be able to stop him	Make him angry, more violent or aggressive, could get more hurt, take longer, get killed
C	Yell for help	May get him to stop if he thinks others know what he's doing, others might help	Make him angry, more violent or aggressive, may get more hurt, could drag me into more secluded area or farther away, could get killed, bystanders don't always help anyway
D	Get away	Could get away, find others to help	Make him angry, more violent or aggressive, may get more hurt, could get killed
E	Call 911	Might scare him into stopping, may get help	Make him angry, more violent or aggressive, he could take or break my phone, may get more hurt, could get killed

difficult or impossible. For example, she recalled that she had left her phone inside the bar with her friend, so she crossed that out as an option because it was not available to her at the time. In addition, Charmaine described the man who assaulted her as being much bigger and stronger than her, so it was not likely she could have fought him off effectively. In fact, she even remembered trying to resist, yelling at him to stop and trying to get out of his grip, but this made him more aggressive and threatening. She also recalled the loud music and crowd noises from inside the bar made it unlikely anyone would have heard her yelling. After reviewing all this information she had at the time, Charmaine made some changes to her justification analysis, as depicted in Table 4.2.

I asked Charmaine which option was the best of all the options available to her at the time—in other words, which option's pros outweighed its cons. She admitted that while the option she chose may have been less than ideal, it was the least bad option out of all the other bad options. Therefore, she concluded that she had chosen the best option.

This scenario is quite common. When we experience a threat, our fight–flight–freeze survival mechanism automatically turns on. It's important to remember that the action our safety mechanism selects is going to be the one that will increase our chance of survival. It does this by quickly assessing the situation, the context, our ability and training, and what has helped us stay alive in similar past situations. And it is pretty darn good at this job. It is not concerned about whether we want to choose fight, flight, or freeze or how we'll feel about what we did or didn't do. But we often feel bad about these behaviors when we don't fully consider the options we had at the time.

When the threat is interpersonal violence, especially when a perpetrator is overpowering in terms of strength or stature, a freeze response is typically the best option. Freezing will make it more likely that we survive (precisely due to the cons that come with fighting or fleeing, as Charmaine identified; these options often instigate more aggression and violence by a perpetrator who wants to maintain control over someone). Even if Charmaine decided she liked the pros and cons ratio of another option better, that option might not have been available to her anyway because she was under threat. This means that her survival mechanism would have activated the

TABLE 4.2. Charmaine's Revised Justification Analysis

	Options	Pros	Cons
A	Do nothing	May get less hurt if I don't resist or confront him, over with faster	Get assaulted, hurt
B	Fight back	May be able to stop him	**I tried, and that just made him angry and more violent and aggressive.** Could get more hurt, take longer, get killed
C	Yell for help	May get him to stop if he thinks others know what he's doing, others might help	Make him angry, more violent or aggressive, may get more hurt, could drag me into more secluded area or farther away, could get killed, bystanders don't always help anyway. **Probably no one could hear me.**
D	Get away	Could get away, find others to help	**I tried, and that just made him angry and more violent and aggressive.** May get more hurt, could get killed
E	~~Call 911~~	~~Might scare him into stopping, may get help~~	~~Make him angry, more violent and aggressive, he could take or break my phone, may get more hurt, could get killed~~

option it decided would be most likely to keep her alive and not the option Charmaine would necessarily feel better about later.

Felipe similarly experienced guilt and shame for what he initially described as "doing nothing" when students at school teased and harassed him. By reviewing his options at the time, he could identify his freezing response as the best of all possible options in many scenarios, as Charmaine did. Like Charmaine, he was smaller and weaker than most of his perpetrators, and he was also outnumbered. Moreover, as described in Chapter 1, human beings depend on others for survival. We have a better chance of surviving when we have reliable caretakers and social groups that can help protect us and get our needs met. This is especially true for younger people. Kids are even less likely than adults to survive on their own without social connections, so it is adaptive for them to do what they can to belong to social groups.

Equipped with this information, Felipe conducted justification analyses for some of the times he was being bullied, and each time, he found that he responded in the best way he could, given the information, resources, and abilities he had at the time. He recalled that he would not likely have been able to fight or flee effectively, as he wished he had. In fact, he remembered attempting to do so on a few occasions at first, and this made things worse, as did telling one of the schoolyard monitors. He was then threatened more. By allowing himself to remember more of the details of the incidents, he came to see that out of the options available to him at the time, his "inaction" was the best one because it minimized his chances of getting further hurt or ostracized.

Paradoxically, Felipe also reported guilt and shame for fighting later in life when he was older and stronger. He placed himself in the impossible position of being damned if he did and damned if he didn't. In choosing to think more carefully about his experiences, Felipe realized at least some of his conclusions must be incorrect because he had these two beliefs that were completely at odds with each other. He initially found thinking and talking about his experiences difficult, as most of us would, because doing so brought up strong aversive feelings such as guilt and shame. But his willingness to feel them anyway allowed him to evaluate his past decisions and behaviors more accurately, which resulted in the dissipation of his guilt and shame.

WRITING EXERCISE: EVALUATE THE OPTIONS YOU HAD

Take some time to check your belief that you did the wrong thing or could and should have done something different. Use Worksheet 4.1 to conduct a justification analysis for each thought in this IJ pile, and reread the relevant sections as needed. You can download and save or print the worksheet from https://www.apa.org/pubs/books/transform-your-guilt-shame (see the Resources tab).

After you have completed your justification analysis, go back to Worksheet 3.1 and summarize what you learned by writing any new conclusions you come to based on all the facts you just reviewed. This could look like the following:

> I made the best decision, given the information, ability, and resources I had at the time.

It's helpful to go through this process even if you didn't identify any thoughts you think belong in this pile. Sometimes, we discover that we did believe we weren't fully justified in doing what we did, even though we never put it in those words. Also, remember you can practice going through these steps if you have thoughts that belong in this pile that are not related to any trauma or adversity. This will help build your resilience against problematic guilt and shame in the future.

WORKSHEET 4.1. Justification Analysis

1. Write down the possible options you had at the time.
2. Cross out any option that was not available to you because you did not think about it at the time or you did not have the necessary information, skills, or resources to act on it.
3. List the pros and cons you considered at the time.
4. Find the option that had the most compelling pros and least impactful cons. That was your best, most justifiable option.

	Options	Pros	Cons
A			
B			
C			
D			
E			
F			

CONCLUSION

Sometimes, people start noticing some loosening of the nonadaptive guilt and shame (NAGS) cycle and feel some relief at this point. But often, this process is like trying to get a tough stain out—we need to wash, rinse, and repeat a few times before we can see what the fabric looks like underneath. However, you don't need to have completely replaced your old conclusions with new ones to move to the next chapter. Many guilt and shame conclusions belong to more than one pile. And just like we might need to do different things to get some stains out, it can be helpful to use different strategies to interrupt the NAGS cycle. In the next chapter, we focus on the thoughts that keep you stuck in the NAGS cycle that fall into the responsibility pile.

You can return to this chapter and the previous one as often as needed (such as when your old thoughts tell you that you should have prevented what happened or were not justified in doing what you did). Also, remember to reread all the challenging responses and reminders you have in your Worksheet 3.1 as you continue to develop your new thinking habit.

CHAPTER 5

CHALLENGE YOUR
RESPONSIBILITY THOUGHTS

Another way we get stuck with unhelpful guilt and shame is if we place responsibility on ourselves for something we have little or no control over or if we place all the responsibility on ourselves for something that has multiple contributing factors. This is especially easy to do when we are accountable for the people or things involved (e.g., a supervisor is held accountable for their team's successes and failures, and a parent is accountable for their child's safety). In addition, if we played a role in something that turned out bad, it is easy to blame ourselves for it. Guilt and shame conclusions related to responsibility often sound like the following:

- I am responsible for what happened.
- I caused what happened.
- I am to blame for what happened.
- Something I did or my action or behavior caused it to happen.
- They were under my care or supervision or command when it happened, so it's my fault they were hurt or killed.

Do any of these statements sound like beliefs you have about trauma or adverse events you have experienced? If they are not already on your Worksheet 2.2, add them now. Mark an "R" next to these kinds of thoughts. Again, many thoughts belong to more than one pile, so don't worry if you have already identified them as being one of the previous types of conclusions.

How responsible do you feel for what happened—100% or close to it? If so, you are not alone. Remember that we like to have some sense of control over our lives. And placing responsibility on ourselves when bad things happen makes us think if we can just figure out what we did that caused it, we can figure out how to prevent it from happening again. On top of that, certain contexts and circumstances make it practically inevitable that someone will become convinced they are responsible for something bad that happens.

HAVING LITTLE OR NO CONTROL

One circumstance that makes it more likely we will attribute undue responsibility to ourselves is, ironically, one in which we have relatively less control or power. **Felipe** provides a good illustration of this. By allowing himself to think about the discrimination and bullying he experienced and the context in which it occurred, he came to understand that some of his internalized guilt and shame came from what he learned from his parents. His indigenous Guatemalan immigrant parents had adopted a survival strategy that is common in minoritized groups, and they passed it on to their child. Felipe was taught not to focus on things he had little or no control over (e.g., racism and discrimination) and instead to focus on what he did have control over: his own behavior. This approach is often adopted by individuals from disenfranchised groups because it alleviates the sense of helplessness that can come from the realization that one has little or no control or power to change their status or how others treat them. Feeling helpless and lacking control is scary and distressing for most people. Focusing instead on what we do have control over, our own behavior, gives us a sense of agency and empowerment, which feels much better.

People from marginalized communities have relatively less power to influence external powers and systems, so it is not surprising that the desire to find ways to regain a sense of control is even more compelling within these groups. The problem is that when we create this false sense of control, we can blame ourselves for things that are not our fault, and this leads to experiencing chronic and problematic guilt and shame and the suffering that comes with it. In Felipe's case, having learned this cultural survival mechanism from his parents, he was quick to assume it was his fault or he deserved it when he was being bullied. This contributed to the snowball effect that is the nonadaptive guilt and shame (NAGS) cycle, where his feelings of guilt and shame just grew in intensity and frequency and easily generalized to increasingly different situations. When he started therapy, Felipe reported alternating between apologizing for things that weren't his fault, such as when he accidentally bumped into someone on a crowded street or if he disagreed with someone, and overreacting with anger when others accidentally did the same. Felipe was stuck in a spiral of shame, withdrawal, anger, and aggression.

WHEN THE TRAUMA CONFLICTS WITH YOUR IDENTITY

Another contextual factor that contributes to our sense of responsibility when something bad happens is the extent to which an identity we hold clashes with reality. Let me explain. We all have a certain view of ourselves. Sometimes these identities are self-ascribed, sometimes they are pushed on us by others, and often there's a little bit of both going on. There's nothing wrong with identities in and of themselves. They are like any other shortcut our brain creates to help us efficiently navigate the world. But a problem can arise when we are too fused with an identity and something happens that challenges the characteristics we have ascribed to that identity. For example, in many parts of the world, a traditional masculine identity is characterized by strength, power, control, and self-reliance. Other identities are also largely defined by these characteristics, such as the strong Black woman archetype and military membership.

Being the victim of trauma or adversity is incompatible with this kind of identity and results in internal conflict that adds to any distress caused by the situation itself. To get some relief, something has to shift: our understanding of what happened or our beliefs about who we are. For most of us, the quicker and easier route is to change our interpretation of what happened to fit our sense of self rather than go through what feels like an identity crisis. In the short term, it is less distressing to hold ourselves responsible for one bad situation and maintain our beliefs about being powerful and having control than to accept that we can be helpless and vulnerable, can't control everything, and fall short of our self-identity. Unfortunately, this short-term benefit of reducing our distress keeps us stuck in the NAGS cycle in the long term because of inaccurate conclusions of responsibility.

What is more beneficial in the long term is to come to more accurate perspectives, even if this means feeling some distress in the short term as you question entrenched identities and come to terms with the reality that it is impossible for anyone to single-handedly have absolute power and control over everything. It might seem difficult at first, but you can reassess and define the identities that serve you best. We all do this throughout our lives. Most likely, you remember doing this when you were a teenager. It can feel rocky to be sure, but you can do it again now and as many times as needed.

CONFUSING ACCOUNTABILITY WITH RESPONSIBILITY

Even outside these circumstances and contexts, it is still common for us to take responsibility and blame ourselves for something we cannot control. A big reason for this is that we confuse responsibility in the sense of accountability with having control. For example, as a supervisor of several faculty members, I am responsible for their performance in my program. I need to monitor their teaching quality, provide feedback, and request improvement plans if needed. If student evaluations indicate that a faculty member is not showing up to class or is not being fair in their grading, I am responsible for assessing and addressing the situation. Because these actions are part of my job, I am accountable. However, would it be accurate to say it is my fault if a faculty member is a bad teacher? I may have some power to change things and work toward improving this faculty member's teaching or replacing them, but ultimately, I don't have control over what this or any other faculty member does or does not do. Wish as I might, I don't have any superpowers to make other people do what I want them to do. Yes, I am responsible for doing something about unacceptable faculty behavior, but I am not responsible for their unacceptable behavior.

Maxwell, my combat vet client who was stuck in the NAGS cycle because he convinced himself he failed to prevent something he had foreseen, was also plagued by guilt and shame because of this confusion between accountability and blame. He was platoon sergeant, so he was responsible for the troops under his command who were all there with him on that street corner where the rocket-propelled grenade exploded. That he was responsible for the lives of those under his command was ingrained in him from day one. But does this mean their deaths and injuries were his fault? He would certainly have been held accountable for doing whatever he could to ensure the safety of his soldiers, to do his best in training and applying what he learned in the field, to stay alert and follow protocol and orders, and to administer commands accordingly. But no one could have rightfully concluded he was to blame for the deaths and injuries that occurred from an enemy act of war he had no control over. Nothing in his training, experience, leadership, or protocols gave him or anyone else complete control over the enemy's actions.

If having such control were possible, the war would not have lasted as long as it did. His superiors continued to tell him he was responsible for his soldiers' lives, but none accused or blamed him for the deaths and injuries of his soldiers on that terrible day because being accountable is not the same as having control over others or being at fault.

Similarly, first responders and medical professionals are responsible for saving lives, but it's not necessarily their fault if one of the people under their care dies. This only sounds contradictory if we confuse responsibility with having control over something. But remember these two things are not the same. When we say a physician is responsible for their patients' lives, we mean that we expect them to put every effort into their training and then into implementing what they learned to the best of their ability so they can save lives. But we know they don't have control over everything that can contribute to whether a patient gets sick or lives or dies. Inevitably, some will die. Blaming a physician for their patients' deaths just because they were responsible for them would be unreasonable and unfair. Sometimes, the cancer doesn't care what or how much treatment you throw at it. Sometimes, the bullet has caused too much damage. Sometimes, there are underlying conditions that no one ever knew were there. Just because you are responsible for making sure something bad doesn't happen does not mean it's your fault if it does.

It is reasonable for us to want leaders, rescuers, and medical professionals to take seriously the safety of those under their command or care. We want them to take responsibility for doing their best, given their options, ability, and resources, and to work to continue improving those. However, it would be unrealistic and unreasonable for us to automatically blame them if something bad happens because that would mean assuming they can 100% control people and things.

PLAYING A ROLE: BEING A DOMINO

Finally, we tend to find it easy to blame ourselves when we play any kind of role in the events that occurred before or during a trauma. This makes sense, right? If I'm hiking on an incline, and I step on a rock that gets dislodged and rolls down the hill and hits and hurts a person hiking below me, I will be more likely to feel guilty than if I was just sitting there and the rock tumbled down without my having touched it. If I hadn't dislodged the rock with my foot, it wouldn't have tumbled down toward the other hiker. But does that mean I'm responsible in the sense that it's my fault the other hiker got hurt? No, I'm not. But I will still be more likely to feel guilt and shame if I played this role—something I did caused something else to happen. This is the case even if what I did is only loosely or indirectly connected to the bad outcome—if instead, the rock I kicked hit a small dead tree branch, which broke off and fell beside a snake resting there, which caused it to leap up and bite the other hiker. I am still susceptible to feeling guilty about the snake hurting that hiker because I had a role in the series of events that resulted in that snake lunging at and biting the hiker.

Did the last scenario remind you of that pastime where you stack dominoes in a row and watch them all topple one at a time after you push the first one toward the next? If you have never seen this in action, you can do a quick search on the internet where you will find thousands of videos of this. It can be useful to think of this domino effect when thinking of how you might be confusing having a role in something with being at fault. What would you say if I asked you who or what is responsible for the last piece in a stack of dominos going down? Many respond to this question by saying the person who pushed the first domino in the stack is responsible. Others say it's the second to last domino in the stack—the one that directly touched and knocked over the last one. But what if any one of the dominoes were removed from the line or not placed just right? Or what if someone knocked over the first domino before all the other dominoes were stacked up? What would happen then? The last domino in the line would not fall, nor would the second to last one. So, who or what is responsible for that last piece falling? All the pieces have to be in the right place at the right time and affect one another in the right way for the last piece to fall.

Let's apply this logic to my hiking scenario. What if the branch that the rock hit had been stronger and didn't fall and scare the snake, or the snake had not been in that exact spot when the branch fell, or the other hiker had stopped a little earlier to tie their shoe and wasn't on the trail below me when I kicked the rock? That hiker would have likely completed their hike unscathed. So, who or what was responsible for the hiker getting the scare of their life? The correct answer is the whole series of unfortunate events that no one intended or could have foreseen or prevented. Feeling momentary guilt or shame about this event will make me ponder this question, and if I can accurately answer it, those feelings will dissipate. Using the domino effect as a metaphor can help us evaluate our estimation of the responsibility we attribute to ourselves. NAGS comes about when we place too much responsibility on ourselves for something that has multiple contributing factors. In many cases, we place all the responsibility on ourselves. The following example illustrates how we can use the domino effect to catch and correct any misattribution of responsibility keeping us stuck in a NAGS cycle.

Some of **Saj's** guilt- and shame-inducing beliefs fell into the responsibility pile. When she first started therapy, she would say that she was 100% responsible for the domestic violence she experienced and for allowing her son to be exposed to it. After we discussed the domino effect, I asked her to consider all the "dominos" that contributed to her domestic violence. We made a table in which she listed all the possible contributing factors and assigned them a percentage of responsibility.

At this point, I encourage my clients to brainstorm and not worry about knowing if something definitely contributed or being accurate with their math. When guilt and shame have been holding the reins for a while, we can get stuck in a loop where our mind makes up stories to make sense of the guilt and shame ("I feel guilt, so I must have done something wrong"), and those stories keep reinforcing the feelings of guilt and shame and so on until those stories seem like reality. And it becomes hard even to consider that there may be other interpretations or ways of thinking. Therefore, it is often necessary to do whatever we can to invite in and allow new thoughts.

In Saj's case, it took her a bit of time and a bit of thinking, but she was able to identify a pretty long list of things that contributed to her partner abusing her. Table 5.1 shows what her list looked like. Of course, she started with herself, as most people do. She didn't assign 100% responsibility to herself as she had before we discussed the domino metaphor, but she still assigned herself a large percentage of responsibility. She was also able to identify many other important contributing factors and assigned a good deal of responsibility to those, too.

Take another look at Saj's table of contributing factors, or dominos. Did you notice that she did not identify her abusive partner as having any responsibility until she was quite a way in? This is common. Clients who have been abused don't often think of assigning any responsibility to the perpetrator at all until I ask them point-blank about it, which is what I had to do with Saj. When I did, she dropped her pen and gasped as she lifted her gaze from her list to look at me. She softly laughed at herself, shaking her head side to side as she added her abusive partner to the list. She couldn't believe she hadn't thought of her partner's responsibility for the abuse. Once she had spent a good amount of time adding all the contributing factors she could think of, we totaled up her assigned percentages, which came to 1,190. Then, we calculated the relative

TABLE 5.1. Saj's Contributing Factors

Contributing factor	Assigned %
Me	90%
No money, nowhere to go	90%
Afraid	80%
Son (loved partner, provided for him)	80%
Ashamed to let others know or ask for help	70%
Not wanting to let anyone know and "give haters another reason to hate lesbians"	50%
Believed it wouldn't last, partner would stop, she would be able to make things better	80%
Felt numb, didn't feel real	80%
Didn't want it to be real	85%
Self-doubt, making excuses	90%
Deserved it (for arguing even when I knew she was in a bad mood, for complaining about small things, for not leaving sooner)	90%
Learned helplessness, frozen	75%
Abusive partner	95%
Partner's external stressors (job, parents, homophobia)	70%
Alcohol	65%
Total	1,190%

responsibility of each item—the proportion of responsibility out of 100%. For example, for "Me," the relative contribution was 90 out of 1,190, or 7.6% (90 divided by 1,190 equals 0.076). Table 5.2 shows the computed relative contributions for each item on Saj's list.

This allowed Saj to see that rather than the 90% of responsibility she initially assigned to herself for the abuse, her responsibility could only be less than 10%. In addition, when she saw the resulting percentage of responsibility on her partner, she realized that she had grossly underestimated that. She decided that much more responsibility should have been assigned to the abuser than any of the other contributing factors, which further reduced the relative responsibility of all the other things on the list, including Saj's own level of responsibility. She said that conducting this responsibility analysis helped clear some of the fog caused by NAGS that was making it hard for her to see things as they were. She said she felt like a weight was gradually being lifted off her shoulders the more she let herself challenge the inaccurate thinking loop she had been stuck in.

WRITING EXERCISE: CONDUCT A RESPONSIBILITY ANALYSIS

Now it's your turn. Use Worksheet 5.1 to check if your conclusions of responsibility are accurate. Start by answering each of the questions to see if you are confusing accountability with having control, if you took on guilt or shame as a cultural survival strategy or to hold on to an important identity, or if you are confusing playing a role in something with being at fault. Then, list all the contributing factors involved in the trauma or adversity, assign the percentage of responsibility to each, and then calculate their relative contributions. Be sure to include things that could have potentially contributed— it's ok if you don't know for sure. Remember to go through this process to evaluate other things you might feel responsible for if you didn't identify any thoughts you think belong in this pile related

TABLE 5.2. Saj's Contributing Factors, Adjusted to Show Relative Percentage

Contributing factor	Assigned %	Relative %
Me	90%	7.5%
No money, nowhere to go	90%	7.5%
Afraid	80%	6.7%
Son (loved partner, provided for him)	80%	6.7%
Ashamed to let others know or ask for help	70%	5.9%
Not wanting to let anyone know and "give haters another reason to hate lesbians"	50%	4.2%
Believed it wouldn't last, partner would stop, she would be able to make things better	80%	6.7%
Felt numb, didn't feel real	80%	6.7%
Didn't want it to be real	85%	7.1%
Self-doubt, making excuses	90%	7.5%
Deserved it (for arguing even when I knew she was in a bad mood, for complaining about small things, for not leaving sooner)	90%	7.5%
Learned helplessness, frozen	75%	6.3%
Abusive partner	95%	8.0%
Partner's external stressors (job, parents, homophobia)	70%	5.9%
Alcohol	65%	5.5%
Total	1,190%	100%

1. Write down all the "dominos" that were involved—all the things that contributed to the bad outcome. This includes any circumstances that you had no control over, as well as things you did have control over. Be sure to include the actions of other people, especially the perpetrator, if there is one!
2. Assign responsibility percentages to each contributing factor (without worrying about the math).
3. Total up all your percentages and write this down in the space provided at the bottom of the Assigned % column.
4. Recalculate the relative contribution of each entry in the table by dividing the percentage you assigned it by the total percentage and write these in the right column.

Factors contributing to the situation	Assigned %	Relative %
Total		

to your traumatic or adverse experiences. Download and save or print additional worksheets from https://www.apa.org/pubs/books/transform-your-guilt-shame (see the Resources tab) as you need. Keep building your new habit of checking for and questioning inaccurate and unhelpful conclusions.

Once you have completed your responsibility analysis, summarize what you learned from it in your Worksheet 3.1 (New, More Accurate, and Helpful Thoughts). This could sound like the following:

> I may have played some role, but my responsibility is much lower than what I have been telling myself. There are at least _____ [*indicate how many you identified*] other contributing factors (e.g., _____ [*list a few important ones here*]), and together, they were responsible in a much bigger way than I was.

> I may have played a role by doing _____, but many other things were as or more responsible than I was.

> I was really at the most responsible _____%, and not the _____% I have been telling myself all this time.

> I may have learned to take on guilt or shame as a cultural survival strategy, to not feel completely helpless, or to maintain my identity, but that doesn't mean I had the power or control I wish I had. It is impossible for me to have total power and control over everything or other people all the time.

> I may have had some responsibility, but that doesn't mean all the other thoughts I've been having about myself (e.g., I'm bad) are true. I need to evaluate those thoroughly, too, before I can come to any accurate conclusion.

CONCLUSION

Blaming ourselves when something bad happens helps us maintain that sense of control we like so much. If it's our fault and we can figure out what we did and not do it again, we can prevent it or other bad things from happening. And when we play any kind of role in a series of events related to something bad happening, it's even easier for our minds to trap us in this false sense of control. But I hope it is increasingly clear that playing a role in something doesn't mean we have control over it, even if we are held accountable.

As with all the steps you've taken so far, it won't hurt to come back to these again a few different times, too. Sometimes, once we open the doors to remembering things we hadn't thought of for a while and allow ourselves to consider alternative ways of thinking, more things come to mind on their own. Remember to keep reviewing your new, more accurate, and more helpful thoughts in Worksheet 3.1. Keep reinforcing your new habit of coming to conclusions based on facts rather than feelings.

CHAPTER 6

CHALLENGE YOUR WRONGDOING THOUGHTS

The next type of guilt and shame conclusion we will tackle is the belief that you did something wrong. This applies to you if your thoughts sound like the following:

- I did something wrong.
- I am to blame.
- It's my fault.
- I am bad, evil, or defective.
- I am a terrible person.
- There's something wrong with me.
- I can't be trusted.

On your Worksheet 2.2, write a "W" next to any thoughts that may belong in this pile. Also, add any thoughts of wrongdoing you may now realize you have or notice as you continue reading this chapter, and mark those with "W," too.

TRUE WRONGDOING REQUIRES WRONG INTENTIONS

Just like the thoughts in the first three piles, we often reach this type of conclusion simply on the basis of a negative outcome. It is easy to judge our behavior as wrong if the outcome is bad. Did you conclude that you must have done something wrong solely based on a bad outcome? If so, that is understandable. But a bad outcome is not sufficient evidence.

For blame or fault to be accurately assigned there needs to be:

1. intention to cause harm, and
2. intention to do something that causes the harm.

Think of the distinction between an accident and murder. In both cases, someone's behavior causes harm. However, with accidents, there is no intention to cause harm, and the behavior was not done intentionally to cause harm. Only in the case of murder is someone deliberately and knowingly engaging in a behavior to intentionally cause harm. So, using the hiking example I introduced in the previous chapter, if the rock I kicked struck and killed the other hiker, that would not be murder. That would be an accident, even if I purposely kicked the rock. We probably have all kicked a rock on purpose at one time or another without any intention to hit or hurt anyone. I know I have—sometimes to move it out of the way and sometimes just for fun to see how far I can get it to go or to hear that satisfying plop sound it makes as it hits water. If I accidentally hit someone with the rock when I don't intend to, it is just that: an accident.

It's still only an accident if I hit someone too hard with a little stone that I just meant to tap them with because I didn't intend to hurt them. Now, if I were acting recklessly and just kicking rocks as hard as I could in every direction knowing there were other people around, then technically, a court of law would be justified in assigning some blame or fault to me even if I didn't have any intention to cause harm to anyone. The term manslaughter (specifically, involuntary manslaughter) is used for this kind of situation when someone is killed by an act that was negligent or reckless and done with disregard, but there was no premeditated intention to cause harm.

If this were the case—that I recklessly kicked a rock that hurt someone—my initial feelings of guilt or shame would be pointing to some truth. This would be a good thing because it would make me want to figure out what I could do differently to avoid feeling these unpleasant emotions in the future. For example, I could decide never again to kick rocks that hard when there is the possibility of others being around. I could also try to mitigate the harm I caused by making amends and helping those I hurt or scared. Having done their job this way, guilt and shame could dissipate naturally.

However, I might condemn myself with guilt and shame by believing and rehearsing thoughts such as, "I should have known better—I should have known I could have hurt someone," or "I must be a bad person for not having thought or cared that I might hurt others." I do have the choice, though, to address these thoughts instead, using the strategies provided in Chapter 3 to remind myself of what was going on and what I did and didn't know at the time. It would be nice to be able to predict all possible negative consequences of my actions before I do them, but as we covered in that chapter, I can't, and neither can you.

WRITING EXERCISE: RECALL YOUR INTENTIONS

Take some time now to recall what your intentions were at the time. To do this, you need once again to let yourself remember the details of the situation in which you think you did something wrong. Reviewing what you wrote in Worksheet 2.1 can be helpful to remind yourself what was going on and what your thoughts and feelings were at the time. If you don't have any thoughts of wrongdoing about that situation, go through these steps for another situation for which you do. As you ask yourself the following questions, don't let any hindsight bias creep in.

- Did you 100% intend to cause something bad to happen?
- Did you 100% intentionally do the behavior that caused something bad to happen?

If you answered no to either of these questions, you are not to blame or guilty of causing the bad thing to happen. Write that down on your Worksheet 3.1 as well as what your intentions were at the time. The following is a suggestion for what you might write on your Worksheet 3.1.

I did not intentionally do _____ to cause what happened.
I just wanted _____ to happen.

If you answered yes to either or both questions about your intention, read on. The rest of this chapter will help you evaluate what you might be telling yourself about what that means. You will find the next section helpful if you have intentionally wanted to hurt someone or cause trouble.

WHAT IF I INTENDED TO CAUSE HARM?

Let's face it, we're all human. None of us are perfect. Most, if not all, of us have acted recklessly or negligently or intended to cause harm at one time or another. In these cases, our feelings of guilt and shame were elicited to help us learn from our error so we could do better moving forward. Our feelings of guilt and shame would have no need to stick around beyond that. However, if we got stuck in a nonadaptive guilt and shame (NAGS) cycle, we may still suffer from guilt and shame long past their usefulness.

For example, it is common to get hooked by thoughts such as, "I must be a bad person for not caring that I might hurt others or intentionally wanting to cause harm." Like so many thoughts we have that come out of trauma and adversity, this conclusion is almost never 100% accurate. Why we do or don't do something is rarely a simple matter—there are so many contributing factors to any behavior that we tend to overlook or forget about. Therefore, before you accurately conclude that you are a bad person, you need to consider everything that contributed to your actions.

WRITING EXERCISE: RECALL THE REASONS FOR YOUR ACTIONS

Let's do that now. It is important that you be honest with yourself about the facts of the situation to come to an accurate conclusion. Remember that the more accurate your conclusions, the more you interrupt the NAGS cycle, take back the reins, and choose your direction. Moreover, operating with more accurate conclusions is like having a more accurate map, so you are more likely to arrive at your desired destinations. To get an accurate map, you're not being asked to put on rose-colored glasses and convince yourself of something that might make you feel better in the moment, but is not accurate either. I'm not trying to get you to come to the conclusion that you're perfect, you've never done anything wrong, or you are not responsible for anything bad that's ever happened. I hope you are beginning to appreciate that reality is not so black and white—things are rarely all or none. I especially hope you realize your feelings may serve you well by eliciting initially adaptive responses but that they are not facts.

In Worksheet 6.1, list all the factors that contributed to your actions. What led you to make the decisions you made and to take the actions you took that you have been telling yourself were wrong or you have been using as proof that you're a bad person? What past experiences, environments, and contexts may have contributed

Write down everything that contributed to your actions, even the small things. Answer the following questions to get you started.

- Was there a series of events that led to your actions?
- Might you have thought, felt, or acted differently if you had different past experiences?
- Might you have thought, felt, or acted differently if the environment had been different?
- Was your fight–flight–freeze response activated?
- Was avoidance or dissociation activated?
- Did you have any alcohol, street drugs, or over-the-counter or prescribed medication in your system that might have influenced your behavior? If so, what led you to take the substance? Were you trying to ease some physical or emotional pain? Were you addicted?
- Did your body respond reflexively to unwanted touching or experiences?

Factors contributing to my thoughts, feelings, and behaviors

to your thoughts, feelings, and behaviors? Conjuring up the domino metaphor again can be helpful here. The set of dominos you are identifying now differs from what you listed in Worksheet 5.1, though there may be some overlap. In that worksheet, you identified all the dominos that contributed to the traumatic or adverse event. You are now identifying all the things that contributed to your actions that you continue to feel shame and guilt about. In other words, what are all the dominos that had to be lined up just right for you to do what you did?

It is possible that if even just one domino were missing, you wouldn't have done the thing you think you did wrong? What if you had different past experiences, or the environment or context you were in had been different—might your life have taken a different turn? Might you have made different decisions or acted differently? If you answered "yes" or even "maybe" to any of these questions, that means there are some reasons you did what you did besides the negative judgments you have been making about yourself.

Most of us are not used to thinking about everything that may have contributed to how we think, feel, or behave. Identifying all the possible contributing factors can be especially challenging, given that our behaviors can be at least in part determined by habit, reflexes, and mind-altering substances or conditions, and we don't often recognize this. Let's consider the most common contributing factors to our behaviors so you can see if any might apply to you that you can add to your Worksheet 6.1.

IMPORTANT DOMINO #1: FIGHT–FLIGHT–FREEZE RESPONSE

One important domino that contributes to our behavior but is often overlooked when we come to conclusions that keep us stuck in a NAGS cycle is how our brains respond to threat. As we know, the fight–flight–freeze response is automatically activated when we perceive a threat, and it is important to consider whether this safety mechanism was activated because it only has three options: fight, flight, or freeze. This means some behaviors are not entirely in our hands and determining our true intention is not always clear-cut.

When **Felipe** started experiencing bullying and discrimination when he was younger, his safety mechanism triggered the freeze response. This made the most sense because he was less powerful than the bullies. Attempting to fight back or flee, in all likelihood, would have been futile and may even have made things more dangerous for him. As Felipe got older and became bigger and stronger, his survival mechanism activated the fight response in some situations. On other occasions, it was still in Felipe's best interest to freeze, though, like when the perpetrator had some power over him.

It is common to feel bad about what your fight–flight–freeze system chooses. For example, you may tell yourself, "I should have fought back." But that's an inaccurate statement. Your survival mechanism intentionally did not choose fight because that would have reduced your chances of surviving. So, you shouldn't have fought back, as your mind is trying to convince you. You should have done exactly what your survival mechanism prompted you to do because that was determined to be your best bet for surviving out of the only options it has: fight, flight, or freeze.

Another thing about the fight–flight–freeze response that was helpful for Felipe to learn is that it can be triggered when our safety brain perceives a threat, whether or not there is a true imminent danger. It will get triggered when it encounters things that remind it of a past danger, like places, situations, sights, sounds, smells, and so forth, even when those things are not dangerous. Your brain does this when it doesn't know what the true signs of danger were in your past traumatic and adverse experiences, and it doesn't want to take any chances. It would rather play it safe by raising a false alarm than risk serious harm or death. As your safety system learns more about what is a true sign of danger and what is not, it will raise fewer false alarms, which can take some time. When we have experienced past trauma or adversity that is not resolved, and we are already stuck in posttraumatic stress disorder (PTSD) or the NAGS cycle, we are more likely to perceive a threat when it is not there.

That's what was happening to Felipe for a long time. Whenever there was the slightest hint of someone disapproving of him—like if someone offered to give him constructive feedback, looked at him without smiling, or just disagreed with something he said—his brain would perceive it as a threat, and he would get defensive and often get into verbal arguments, which sometimes escalated into physical fights. To be sure, Felipe still encountered true threats sometimes, for which the activation of his fight–flight–freeze response was helpful. However, he also noticed occasions of minimal or low threat for which his response was overblown and heightened his risk of getting hurt.

Take a moment to consider whether the fight–flight–freeze response was one of the contributing factors to your behavior. If it was, write it down in Worksheet 6.1.

IMPORTANT DOMINO #2: AVOIDANCE OR DISSOCIATION

When we are already stuck in PTSD or a NAGS cycle, we may also be experiencing other things that contribute to our behavior, like avoidance. As we have already covered, we sometimes need to avoid being fully conscious of what is going on around us to survive, like when we need to remain unaware that someone is abusing us when we are dependent on them. And it's difficult to be precise and pick and choose what we avoid. This means that when we are in avoidance mode, it is usually generalized across different aspects of our lives. When avoidance is activated, we don't have full access to our true wants and desires, decision-making power, abilities, or information. You may have heard this kind of unawareness being called *dissociation*. However it shows up and whatever we call it, it is important to consider if avoidance or dissociation may have been involved in actions we feel guilt and shame about.

Take a moment to consider whether avoidance or dissociation was one of the dominoes that contributed to your behavior. If it was, write it down in Worksheet 6.1.

IMPORTANT DOMINO #3: ALCOHOL AND DRUGS

Many recreational and prescribed substances can influence our thoughts, feelings, and behavior, and their effects are often overlooked when we come to conclusions that keep us stuck in a NAGS cycle. If you had any alcohol, street drugs, or over-the-counter or prescribed medication in your system when you did something you are feeling guilt and shame about, write this in your Worksheet 6.1, and describe the ways that the substance may have influenced your behavior.

It is also easy for us to get stuck with NAGS about having used alcohol or another substance in the first place. This often sounds like the following:

- If I hadn't been drunk or high, the bad thing wouldn't have happened.
- It's my fault because I was drunk or high.
- I deserved it because I was drunk or high.

Charmaine blamed herself in lots of different ways for being sexually assaulted by the guy she met at the bar. In addition to the ways I have already described, she also convinced herself that it wouldn't have happened if she hadn't been drinking. She believed this so much so that she stopped drinking altogether for many years. And later, when she drank to numb some of her pain, she did it alone at home. Conducting the first three analyses (foreseeability and preventability [Chapter 3], justification [Chapter 4], and responsibility [Chapter 5]) helped her shed some of the inaccurate guilt and shame she placed on herself. But she continued to believe that her drinking, at least in part, contributed to the assault. She kept telling herself that she would not have been assaulted if she had not been drunk—that he wouldn't have targeted her if she hadn't been drinking as much, that she would have been able to know the man who assaulted her was up to no good and wouldn't have gone outside with him, and that she would have been able to get away.

I asked her to consider what nice, caring people, including her, are compelled to do when they are around someone who doesn't have their full wits about them (either because of drugs or alcohol or any other reason). Does it make her want to assault or otherwise take advantage of the incapacitated person? Or does it compel her to try to help, take care of, or protect them? A look of realization crept across her face as she slowly nodded and firmly stated that, of course, she would not want to hurt or take advantage of them. She would maybe even want to help in some way to make sure they were safe. This reminded her that the blame belonged to the perpetrator who chose to abuse her and not to her for drinking. Of course, she could also decide drinking too much may put her at increased risk of making decisions that are not in her best interest and being less able to defend herself if she needed to, and therefore, choose to drink more moderately and to make pacts with friends she is out with not to leave each other alone if one of them becomes intoxicated. But that would not mean she would be to blame if someone chose to hurt her while she did drink or even became intoxicated.

If you have guilt and shame because of your use of alcohol, street drugs, or over-the-counter or prescribed medication, ask yourself what led you to take the substance in the first place. Write down all the reasons you can think of in your Worksheet 6.1. Consider the following questions as you do so. Did you choose to take a mind-altering substance so you would do what you did? If not, why did you drink or take the substance? Did you choose to become addicted or dependent on the substance? If not, what are the experiences that led to the habit? Were you taking something to help ease or avoid some physical or emotional pain? On Worksheet 6.1, be sure you include all the dominos that may have led you to take the substance when you did.

IMPORTANT DOMINO #4: HARDWIRED PHYSICAL RESPONSES DURING A SEXUAL ASSAULT

Besides the fight–flight–freeze response, we have other hardwired systems that are automatically triggered under specific circumstances. One of these reflexive systems is a particularly common contributor to unwarranted guilt and shame in people who have had unwanted sexual experiences: We experience sexual arousal and pleasure when erogenous zones are touched. The most well-known of these body parts are genitals and breasts, but there are a few others, and they can vary from person to person. When these areas of the body are touched, a host of physical changes are triggered, such as increased heart rate, increased blood flow and sensitivity to the sexual organs, vaginal lubrication, penile erection, and orgasm. In addition, the brain releases neurotransmitters and hormones that produce pleasure (dopamine), giddiness and euphoria (norepinephrine), and feelings of attachment and love (oxytocin). Just like the fight–flight–freeze response is automatically triggered like a reflex when a danger is perceived, this sexual response is automatically triggered when erogenous zones are stimulated, whether you want it to happen or not. Many people who have had unwanted sexual contact feel unwarranted guilt and shame because of the sexual arousal and pleasure they experienced.

This certainly was the case for **Charmaine**. She thought she was "bad" for having enjoyed the pleasant sensations she experienced when her father's friend molested her. In addition to the pleasurable physical and emotional reflexes that were triggered during the abuse, she also remembered liking the attention, which was much more than any attention she felt she got from her busy parents. He made her feel special. The pleasure that she experienced was used by her survival mechanism to help her maintain attachment with the perpetrator. Her mind convinced her that her father's friend was being nice, not abusive. This was effective in the service of her survival. But, later, when her mind tried to make sense of this experience, she interpreted her pleasure and lack of confrontation (fighting) or withdrawal (fleeing) as signs that she must have "asked for it," that she must have done something to give him the impression she wanted him to abuse her sexually and that, therefore, she must have been a "sick kid."

Charmaine found it extremely helpful to take some time to consider the role that normal reflexive responses played in her experiences. She came to understand that just because she felt pleasant sensations didn't mean she wanted the perpetrator to abuse her. In fact, once she allowed herself to think about it, she recalled having some sense that it was wrong, doing many things to try to avoid being alone with him, and wishing she could have his attention without having to engage in sexual acts with him. She also came to understand that feeling pleasant sensations or liking the attention didn't mean she was bad. She now understood that her body reacted reflexively to what was happening to it and felt compassion for herself as a child who appreciated the attention.

If you ever had a sexual experience that you did not want or consent to and you feel some guilt or shame due to having pleasant sensations, including orgasm, take some time to write down in your Worksheet 6.1 what you now know about what caused those sensations and what they mean. Consider the following questions as you do so. Did you experience sexual arousal or pleasant emotions because you wanted the perpetrator to do what they did? Or was it because, like all humans, you have reflexive responses to being touched in certain places, whether you want them to occur or not?

REVIEW AND SUMMARIZE

Review the contributing factors you listed in Worksheet 6.1 to challenge your old conclusions of wrongdoing and write more accurate conclusions in Worksheet 3.1. The following are some examples of what my clients' new conclusions sound like:

> I may have preferred to have thought or felt or acted differently, but that doesn't necessarily mean I could or should have or that I did anything wrong. Many things contributed to my feelings, thoughts, and behaviors: _____ [*summarize the most important contributing factors you identified*].

> It is likely that if _____ [*summarize the most important contributing factors you identified*] had not happened or was not triggered, I would probably have acted differently or made different decisions.

If, after conducting some thorough, honest evaluation of your conclusions, you determined that you correctly placed some guilt or shame on yourself, ask yourself the following questions. Given that there are many contributing factors to anyone's behavior, is any action necessarily due to a person's "badness"? Would someone who is all "bad" feel guilt and shame? Doesn't the fact that you feel guilt or shame mean you are a good person with a conscience and important values you aspire to? Does making a mistake in the past have to wholly and permanently define who someone is in the present or future, or are we all imperfect beings just trying to do the best we can with the information, resources, and ability we have?

Summarize your answers to this line of questioning in Worksheet 3.1. The following are representative of how many of my clients have summarized their answers to these questions:

I may have done something wrong, but that doesn't mean
_____ [*fill in the blank with the labels you had given
yourself—for example, I am evil, bad, defective, or a monster;
there's something wrong with me; I can't trust myself*]. Many
things contributed to my behavior (e.g., _____ [*summarize the most important contributing factors you identified*]).

The fact that I have felt guilt and shame about this is evidence
that I have a good conscience, and it is evidence against any
conclusion I might have that I am evil, bad, or a monster.

Now that I am aware of the things I have control over and
those I don't, I can make different choices about the things
I have control over. Staying in the NAGS cycle will not allow
me to do that. Instead, I can use my feelings of guilt and shame
adaptively and let them take their natural course.

CONCLUSION

To summarize, many situations and circumstances can contribute
to our feelings, thoughts, and behaviors: being in fight–flight–freeze
mode, having to maintain an attachment to a person or institution
or experiencing avoidance or dissociation for other reasons, being
under the influence of some substance, or experiencing normal physical reflexes. These and other factors are more likely to control our
behaviors than our will or intention under certain circumstances. We
need to consider whether any of these things were involved before
we can conclude that we did something wrong. And if, after a thorough evaluation, we find we did do something wrong and made
mistakes, we don't have to let our minds convince us that this means
something indelible about our goodness and worth, like that we are
bad or evil. In fact, doing so will make it more likely that we do things
we feel guilt and shame about. In the next chapter, we evaluate your
beliefs about violating your important values.

CHAPTER 7

CHALLENGE YOUR VIOLATED VALUES THOUGHTS

The final pile of common guilt and shame conclusions we will address has to do with our belief that we did something that went against some important value, moral, or personal standard of what is right. You have thoughts that belong to this pile if they sound anything like the following:

- I did not uphold my principles, values, morals, or conscience.
- I violated my principles, values, morals, or conscience.
- I went against values important to my community, culture, group, or society.
- I did not meet a personal standard.
- I did something wrong and am to blame.

If they are not already on your Worksheet 2.2, add the thoughts you think apply to you and mark all the thoughts you think belong to this pile with a "V."

Now, let's evaluate whether your thoughts are 100% true. You may be surprised to learn that even when you acted in opposition to one value, you were almost certainly acting in support of another. It is helpful to understand a little more about values and how they operate in our lives to evaluate our conclusions about whether we upheld our values.

DEFINING VALUES

Values are our principles, standards of behaviors, judgments about right and wrong, and what we want to stand for. Values have four characteristics that, if we don't explicitly consider, can contribute to some nonadaptive guilt and shame (NAGS) thoughts in the violated values pile:

1. Values are individualistic.

   What is important to me may not be important to you, and vice versa. We might have shared societal and cultural values, but not all our values will be the same.
2. Values are dynamic, not static.

   What is important to me at one time in my life may not be important in the same way at a different time in my life.
3. We don't have just one value; we have many.

   We have values in different domains of our lives. We have values that guide our behavior in romantic partnerships, friendships, and family relations. We have values related to finances, employment, and education. We have values related to our health and well-being and that of our communities and the environment.
4. We prioritize different values in different contexts at different times.

   Sometimes, we have different values that can even be at odds with each other in certain contexts. For example, let's say I have a value of spending quality time with my child and being an inclusive leader at work. To live according to these values, I can only effectively prioritize one at a time. When I am at work, I will be most effective at living my value if I am fully present, paying attention and listening to my staff and considering different options in a thoughtful manner. Focusing on my parenting value at the same time might interfere with my effectiveness as a leader. The same is true the other way around. I would not be effectively living my value of spending quality time with my child if I were trying to solve some work problem at the same time as I'm playing a game with them.

We need to take into account this information about values if we are to properly evaluate the accuracy of any conclusions we might have about whether we violated them. Let's turn to some case examples to illustrate this point.

CASE EXAMPLE OF CONCLUSION OF VIOLATED VALUES

One of the biggest sources of guilt and shame for **Saj** was that her son was exposed to the intimate partner violence perpetrated by her partner. One specific instance especially induced a belief that she had done something wrong. She recalled an argument that culminated in her spouse holding her up against a wall by her neck and Saj yelling out their son's name, which prompted him to come into the room. Feeling bad that he had to witness this abuse, Saj quickly concluded that she must be feeling guilty and ashamed because she did something wrong. Because she did all she could to avoid these feelings, she did not allow herself to challenge this belief. Instead, the feelings festered, and she became increasingly convinced that she was a bad mother for causing her son emotional distress by exposing him to the abuse (and possibly to her death). Being a loving and caring mother and protecting her son from harm were important values to Saj. She could not reconcile these values with having called for him and putting him in harm's way, so she assumed she had violated her values and condemned herself to feeling terrible for the rest of her life.

Once she stopped avoiding her memories of the abuse and her feelings and stopped rehearsing the same conclusions, Saj allowed herself to remember a few more important details about that incident and her actions. She recalled having tried several things to get her spouse to release her. She apologized, begged, cried, pulled, pushed, and kicked. All her efforts were to no avail. Saj was much smaller and weaker than her spouse. Any attempts Saj made seemed to make her spouse angrier and tighten up her grip. While recalling all this, Saj also remembered that she called out their son's name in desperation after all else had failed. Her spouse had never seriously physically hurt Saj in front of their son before—she seemed to restrain herself when he was around. So, there was good reason for Saj to think that reminding her partner that their son was home would help her spouse "snap out of" her fit of rage and aggression. And this is exactly what happened. As soon as their son came into the room, her spouse let go of Saj and walked out of the house. After this, Saj decided to leave and pursue legal protection for her and her son.

In reviewing this information, Saj could see how she was acting in line with her values by calling her son when she was being abused. She needed to prioritize staying alive and healthy to be able to be a mother to her son. Her decision to call him did not violate her values of caring for and protecting him but was in service of these values.

CONFLICTING VALUES IN THE WORKPLACE

There are some occupations in which feelings of guilt and shame are an occupational hazard because there will almost certainly be occasions when it is difficult to see that values are being upheld because of competing demands or because some values sometimes conflict with one another. The following two are most familiar to me from the research and my clientele.

Competing Demands in Medical Professionals and First Responders

Many medical professionals and first responders often report experiencing guilt and shame for not having saved everyone from being hurt or killed. Saving people may be part of someone's job, their responsibility, or what they are accountable for. But we know no one person can save everyone, even if they are excellently trained medical professionals. It is inevitable that some people under their care will be gravely injured or die. There are often too many variables involved that are outside of anyone's control. Even with the things we have some control over, we may need to prioritize different values (and, therefore, different actions) at different times.

This was indeed one of **Duri's** sources of guilt and shame. Duri experienced NAGS because of different types of conclusions. They berated themself for having run away so fast during the earthquake—for not having helped more people escape the collapsing building. In addition, some of the people Duri cared for in the field where they had fled to did not survive. Some survived but had injuries that resulted in more debilitating outcomes than if standard care with the necessary resources had been possible. Duri repeatedly told themself that it was their fault that people died and that they should have saved more lives. In other words, they did not live up to their personal and professional values of providing quality care, saving lives, and improving their patients' outcomes.

By now, everything we've covered may allow you to point to some holes in Duri's reasoning. Duri was able to do just that after we started working together. First, they learned about the fight–flight–freeze response, and after recalling the details of the situation, they could accept that they had no other good option but to flee. Had they stayed in the building any longer to try to help others get out, neither they nor their patient would have survived. This would have also meant that Duri would not have been able to help anyone else who escaped and made it to the field or live up to their values.

Next, Duri reviewed everything they did once they made their way to the field. They remembered having to triage the injured and focus on those most in need of care but who also had the best chance of surviving, given the limited resources available. Duri initially only recounted details about the people who died or whose injuries they could not mend perfectly. But once they allowed themself to recall all the details of the situation, Duri recalled having worked nonstop for over 10 hours on the heels of having worked almost 5 hours at the hospital before the earthquake struck. They worked on so many people that they lost count of those who had life-threatening conditions that they were able to stabilize or who recovered fully from their injuries. Duri could finally see how they did act according to their values and that the circumstances were such that it was impossible to save everyone, much less treat everyone perfectly.

It was also impossible to provide ideal bedside care. Some people suffered or even died alone. This was something else Duri felt bad about, which is understandable. But the problem is that Duri interpreted feeling bad with, again, concluding they did not uphold this important value. They had thoughts such as, "I should have done more to make sure no one was left to suffer or die alone." However, in reviewing the facts, Duri remembered they had done what they could in this regard, too. They directed some volunteers to serve in this capacity—to hold hands, talk to, and provide whatever support and comfort they could. Anyone who could helped as much as they were able, but there were not enough people to take care of everything and everyone. Duri ultimately changed their initial conclusion to one that was more accurate: "I did what I could, and all that I did was in line with my values." It was hard for them to see that at first because they could not act on their values with everybody there who needed care at the same time. But that does not mean they were not acting in line with their values at any given time.

Because I am writing this on the heels of the COVID-19 pandemic, I am acutely aware that many medical and caretaking professionals around the world are ridden with guilt and shame because of similar circumstances. Many people suffered and died, and many did so completely alone. At first, no one knew much about the virus or how to prevent or treat it. So, many people were infected, and many could not be effectively treated. In fact, as this book goes to press, we still don't fully understand or know how to treat COVID-19 effectively 100% of the time. Even if we did, that wouldn't mean we could always successfully treat everyone anyway because it would depend on our resources and capacity at the time. There are still shortages in medical facilities, personnel, and equipment in many places to this day. This means the circumstances ripe for developing guilt and shame responses continue.

Posttraumatic distress and guilt and shame in individuals who work in medical and caregiving settings have been documented in several scientific journal articles, the news, and other media. My colleagues and I have also seen this in our clients. Fortunately, we have also witnessed firsthand the shedding of unwarranted guilt and shame in these folks as they learn to challenge their initial conclusions.

Conflicting Values in Military Combatants

All the active duty and veteran clients I have worked with identified valuing human life in some way or another. They each asserted that it was important to them to protect and save others from being hurt or killed. It is not surprising, then, that many experience guilt and shame related to some of the requirements of their job, which can involve hurting or killing others. Does this mean they are violating their values when they do so? Maybe. Or are they valuing life by removing greater threats to life by killing an enemy who poses a threat to the survival of their comrades, family, friends, or other innocents? One could argue that there may be other options than war to resolve conflicts and protect ourselves. But those other options are not often immediately available to folks on the battlefield confronting enemy threats. As we covered in the justification analysis section in the previous chapter, it is not fair or accurate to judge ourselves for not choosing an option that was not available to us at the time. Too often, the only option available on the battlefield is to kill or be killed. And remember, your hardwired survival mechanism will always strongly compel you to do whatever it determines you need to do to stay alive.

This is indeed something that contributed to **Maxwell's** sense of guilt and shame. One of the first things he told me when we started working together was that he felt ashamed for not having saved the lives of the civilians who were killed on the street corner that was blasted. He also felt guilt and shame for having killed some of those who launched the rocket-propelled grenade because he always identified himself as someone who valued human life. It makes sense, therefore, that Maxwell felt bad because people died. And because he has a conscience, the natural feelings of guilt and shame would have prompted him to evaluate the situation to see if there is anything he might learn from it—anything he might try to do differently next time to minimize loss of life. However, the situation was such that he was unable to take the time to do this. Maxwell had to continue to address any possible remaining danger and help maintain security while civilians dispersed to safety, medics cared for the wounded, and plans were being made for their next moves. His feelings of guilt and shame led to uncontested conclusions that he acted against his values.

After that, Maxwell increasingly avoided thinking about this situation because he experienced terrible pangs of guilt and shame whenever he was reminded of it. He also developed posttraumatic stress disorder, a big part of which is avoidance. This avoidance meant that he didn't get to evaluate his quickly laid conclusion that he violated his values. Luckily, Maxwell eventually allowed himself to do this in therapy. First, he named all his values. Then, he reviewed his intentions and identified the values he was acting on when he did each of the things he did on the day the blast went off on that civilian-filled street corner. In doing this, he could see that, in each case, he was acting out one or more of his values.

Maxwell recalled having checked in with his superior officer about his sense of danger before anything happened, partly because he was concerned about the safety of the civilians there. He also agreed with his supervisor that they should not take any action unless they were certain there was danger because doing so could incite aggression from the enemy if they were around, which would put civilians and their troops in harm's way. He was even able to let himself acknowledge that his shooting enemy combatants after they attacked was in line with his values, even though this meant potentially killing some of them, which went against some of his values. This was the only option at his disposal at the time to eliminate the danger they posed to the civilians, his comrades, and himself. His actions were in line with his value of protecting others.

There is another important way that being in a war or experiencing other kinds of longstanding threats can result in behaviors that go against some of our values. Chronic threat exposure can be particularly challenging to our survival systems, and we can end up feeling and acting in ways that seem to go above and beyond what is called for to protect ourselves. This is not an uncommon scenario in times of war. Some people, for example, have reported that they experience guilt and shame for having intentionally killed or hurt someone who was not posing an immediate threat but was associated with or a reminder of the danger they were under in some way. This could be explained by the fight–flight–freeze response being chronically activated, creating a strong desire to eliminate all possible threats. Some people have reported feeling positive emotions when harming others, including intense excitement and joy, and interpreted that as evidence of them being bad. But there is another explanation for this. It is intensely relieving to eliminate a potential threat and the terror that comes with it, and it is not surprising that a feeling of elation can follow. If the threat was eliminated through harming or killing others, we can mistakenly attribute the feeling of pleasure to that harm. But it may simply be due to the elimination of the threat.

WRITING EXERCISE: WHAT VALUES WERE YOU UPHOLDING?

Go back to Worksheet 3.1 and write down the values you were acting in line with before, during, and after the trauma or adversity. Then, write down the things that may have gotten in the way of you living up to some of your values at all times. In other words, did some values need to take the back seat under the circumstances? Remember, just because you had to prioritize one value at the time of the trauma or adversity does not mean you were violating other values.

In addition, ask yourself if it was difficult to access your values at the time of the trauma or adverse event or choose to act on them. As we discussed earlier, when stuck in a NAGS cycle, we can lose touch with what is important to us. And as we went over in the last chapter, many things contribute to our behavior. It is important to consider whether these were at play when you concluded that you violated your values. Was your fight–flight–freeze response activated? Were you already in posttraumatic distress, and avoidance or dissociation was activated? Were you under the influence of alcohol or drugs? Was your body responding reflexively? If you answered yes to any of these questions, you may not have had full access to your values, and/or you could not act in accordance with or against them. Summarize your answers to this line of questioning to develop new, more helpful conclusions in Worksheet 3.1. The following are examples of how some of my clients responded:

> I did uphold some of my values (e.g., _____), even though some (e.g., _____) had to take a back seat.
>
> I had to prioritize my value of _____ over my value of _____.
>
> Just because there were circumstances (e.g., _____) that made it impossible to live according to my value of _____ does not mean that I was violating that value.
>
> I did what I could, and all that I did was in line with my values.
>
> Feeling pleasant emotions when a threat is reduced doesn't necessarily mean I am happy about everything that happened to eliminate the threat.
>
> Being under constant threat wreaked havoc on my survival mechanism and resulted in my perceiving and acting to eliminate threats when they were not there. Now that I know I am no longer under threat (even if I still feel like I am), I take steps to treat my posttraumatic distress, try to repair the damage I have caused, and continue to strive to live according to my values.

If this part of the work is difficult because you don't know what your values are, you are not alone. As I said, it's common for folks to lose touch with their values when they are stuck in a NAGS cycle. That is why, in the next chapter, I provide some strategies you can use to help you identify your values.

CONCLUSION

A common experience in this process is that, as you begin to understand that your guilt and shame conclusions are inaccurate and you develop different perspectives, you can still feel guilt and shame. Remind yourself that this doesn't necessarily mean you are guilty or have anything to be ashamed of. You can just let these emotions be and not get hooked by them. Working through the steps in this and the previous chapters more than once will be helpful in reminding you of this. Also, remember that using the steps to challenge conclusions of guilt and shame that may apply to other situations besides trauma or adversity will help build up your skills and could help prevent NAGS from latching on in the future.

As you continue to chip away at the NAGS piles and they no longer take up so much space in your head and heart, you can focus more on what is around you and what direction you want to take. You can choose what you want your life to be about, how you want to spend your time and engage in activities that bring you fulfillment and joy. When our brains have been cluttered with NAGS piles for some time, we can forget that there is a horizon. We can forget that we have values, that there are paths ahead we can take that will bring us closer to what is truly important to us, and that we might have a choice about the direction we want to take. Whether you feel like you have thoroughly processed and removed the last tough stains from each of your piles of thoughts, going through the next chapter will help you navigate the new horizon that may be starting to peek through for you. The next chapter is also a helpful guide on how to use any guilt and shame based on accurate conclusions more adaptively than staying stuck in the NAGS cycle.

CHAPTER 8

USE GUILT AND SHAME IN AN ADAPTIVE WAY

I hope that by this point you have loosened the grip that nonadaptive guilt and shame (NAGS) has on your life by at least starting to question some of your guilt and shame conclusions, if not outright discarding and replacing the inaccurate beliefs with more accurate and helpful ones. To be clear, I am not suggesting we shouldn't feel guilt or shame if we caused harm or that we excuse all recklessness or intentionally hurtful behavior. One of my primary driving forces as a trauma psychologist and as a human being is to work toward eliminating harmful behavior—toward a world where each of us is more mindful of our actions so we reduce the likelihood of hurting others and ourselves. Therefore, I want people to feel guilt and shame when they act in ways that hurt others. If someone feels guilt or shame for having done something harmful, they are more likely to evaluate the situation, choose different actions that may be less likely to have a negative outcome, and take steps toward repairing the situation or making amends. I also want people to feel guilt and shame before they act in ways that could be harmful. Emotions can be elicited from the mere contemplation of engaging in some actions. We can use these emotions to inform our decisions. Can you imagine what the world would be like if we all used guilt and shame in this adaptive way? How much less hurt and violence would there be in the world?

Therefore, it can be in your best interest to allow yourself to notice and feel guilt and shame as long as you do not unquestioningly believe any conclusion your mind comes up with and turn the feelings into NAGS. You now know that under many circumstances, guilt and shame can lead you to inaccurate, unhelpful conclusions and cause many problems. You know that you can allow yourself to feel these emotions (rather than avoid them) without taking them as conclusive evidence of facts. And you know how to separate your feelings from your thoughts and how to evaluate your guilt and shame thoughts to see whether they are inaccurate or at least based on incomplete information, which is usually the case. And you know that even if you still experience NAGS, you can continue challenging the thoughts that contribute to these feelings using the strategies you practiced in the previous chapters so you can come to more accurate and helpful conclusions. The other beneficial thing about allowing yourself to feel rather than avoid your guilt and shame is that this can connect you with what is important to you: your values. I touched on this topic briefly in the last chapter; here, I will delve into it more deeply.

CONNECT TO YOUR VALUES

Your values are your principles, your judgment of what is important in life, what is right and wrong, and what you want to stand for. You have values for different areas of your life, including family, romance, friendships, work, education, recreation, mental health, physical health, finance, religion or spirituality, and community. And it turns out that living according to your values is integral to your well-being and happiness in the long run. Thankfully, this is the case even if you had long periods of believing inaccurate conclusions of guilt and shame or not living according to your values before deciding to move toward your values.

Let me illustrate how you can use your feelings of guilt and shame (whether based on accurate or inaccurate conclusions) to identify your values using a client example. **Saj** was riddled with guilt and shame for having called out to her son when she was being abused because she believed she violated her value of protecting him from harm. Of course, she knows now that this act was in line with that value under the circumstances. But while she was stuck in the NAGS cycle, Saj had convinced herself she had acted against this value and, therefore, she was a bad mother. This belief only resulted in her acting less in line with her values. She invested more of her time and energy in activities in the service of avoidance, which meant she spent less time with her son, for example. But once she decided to face her feelings of guilt and shame to challenge the conclusions her mind had come to, Saj was able to see that those feelings pointed her to her value of being a caring and protective mother to her son. After doing this work, Saj described feeling lighter, freer, and reconnected with what was important to her. This was directly observable in her increased quality time with her son. By confronting her guilt and shame, Saj was left with a more accurate life map. She had a better sense of the direction in which she wanted to head. And she had a better handle on the reins of the wagon taking her there. No longer were guilt and shame calling the shots for her.

WRITING EXERCISE: IDENTIFY YOUR VALUES

Like Saj, you can review your guilt and shame thoughts and see what important values they point to. Look back at Worksheet 2.2, read each thought you wrote down, and see if it points to a value you thought you had gone against or neglected. As you do so, write down in Worksheet 8.1 anything that sounds like it might be a value, moral, or belief that seems important to you. Values tend to be especially present in thoughts you identified as belonging in the

WORKSHEET 8.1. My Values

Write down any values that seem important to you for each domain of your life.

Family

Romance

Friendships

Work

Education

Recreation

Mental health

WORKSHEET 8.1. **My Values (*Continued*)**

Physical health

Finance

Religious or spiritual

Community

Other:

Other:

Other:

wrongdoing and violated values piles (marked with "W" and "V," respectively). If you notice that any thoughts in Worksheet 2.2 still elicit strong emotion, circle them so you know to come back and work on challenging them some more. But don't get sidetracked by challenging the thoughts right now. Your current task is to find the values underlying your guilt and shame conclusions. For now, see if you can objectively review the old conclusions you had with the sole intention of identifying the values they might point to. Pretending they are someone else's thoughts can help with this.

Like Saj, **Maxwell** also had thoughts that reflected the value of caring for others. He thought he should have done more to prevent the explosion and the harm it created. Likewise, **Duri's** thoughts reflected a value of caring for others—recall that they thought they were bad for not staying to help others. These thoughts indicate that Saj, Maxwell, and Duri deem human life precious and seek to be protectors, helpers, or healers. These thoughts also point to the values of acquiring knowledge, awareness, and preparedness. If these values resonate with you, write them down in Worksheet 8.1.

Maybe you thought you deserved the bad things that happened to you, like **Felipe**, who initially thought something must be wrong with him. Or you may be like **Charmaine**, who came to believe that she must be bad and must have deserved the abuse perpetrated against her. These kinds of beliefs cause distress because they conflict with our values about respecting ourselves and our well-being. Write down the values you have about your physical and mental health in Worksheet 8.1.

You may now have a few values written down, or you may have many. There is no magic number of values you should have. You just have the values you have. It doesn't hurt to keep exploring, though. When we've been stuck in a NAGS cycle, we can lose sight of what matters to us. And it can be a little challenging to get back in touch with what it would look like to live life "our way."

So, keep exploring and write down anything that comes to mind. The following are some tips:

1. Ask yourself the following questions and write down in Worksheet 8.1 the values they help you uncover:
   - If you thought you did something wrong, what is it that you think you did wrong? What was the "right" thing you told yourself you should have done? Why? What about doing that is important to you? What value would this have been in the service of?
   - If you had conclusions about things you "should" have done, why would you have liked to have done that? What value would this have been in line with?
   - If you believed that you were bad or deserving of bad things, write down values about yourself and your well-being these beliefs might have harmed.
   - What do you care about? How do you want to care about this?
   - Who do you care about? How do you want to care about this person?
   - What gets you excited? What are you passionate about? What makes you feel like time stands still? What feels effortless?
   - What feels like a chore, but you want to do it anyway because it's important to you?
   - What are you grateful for? How do you want to live in gratefulness?
   - What things do you do that feel meaningful? What are some things you don't yet do that you think would bring meaning to your life?
2. From the following list of examples, write down any that resonate with you:
   - being assertive and asking for what I need
   - adding beauty to the world

   - having compassion and kindness
   - having patience and persistence
   - being courageous (note that this doesn't mean fearless)
   - treating others fairly and equitably
   - continuing growing, learning, and self-challenging
   - having sincerity and integrity
   - maintaining energy and well-being
   - creating or inventing
   - being playful and appreciating humor
   - maintaining connection and intimacy
   - being open-minded and flexible
   - being responsible and accountable
   - spending quality time with my loved one
   - being there when my loved one needs me

3. Ask others who know you well to tell you what they most admire or appreciate about you and write down any of your values this might reveal.

4. Write down what you would want others you care about to say they admire or appreciate about you even if you don't think they would actually say it.

I suggest you read through the list of prompts repeatedly, thinking about a different area of your life, including family, romance, friendships, work, education, recreation, mental health, physical health, finance, religion or spirituality, and community. You may find that a value in one area seems to be in complete contradiction with a value in another area. That is expected, as we discussed in the previous chapter.

How do you know if the things you have written down are values? Do they feel important to you? Would living according to the things you wrote down feel meaningful to you? Would they be important to you even if no one ever saw them or saw you living up to them? If you answered "yes" to any of these questions or even "maybe," they are probably values.

Once you have identified a handful of values, the next step is finding ways to live your values.

WRITING EXERCISE: TRACK YOUR ACTIVITIES TO LIVE YOUR VALUES

A good place to start is to determine how much of your time you currently spend serving your values. Use Worksheet 8.2 to identify the actions and activities you engage in each week that align with your values. Start with today. Write down everything you did in roughly hour-long blocks. Then continue doing the same each day for at least 1 week. You can use your own paper or digital documents or download more worksheets (https://www.apa.org/pubs/books/ transform-your-guilt-shame; see the Resources tab).

The activity tracking of many clients I have worked with who were stuck in a NAGS cycle for a while initially looked a lot like Duri's first one, shown in Table 8.1. I have shortened and edited it a bit for the sake of clarity.

I provide this example just to give you an idea of what an activity-tracking worksheet might look like. You track everything you do over the course of the day. Yours might look a lot like this one or not at all like it. The point of this exercise is to notice how you spend your time and whether it is serving your values. If you spend a lot of time in the service of only one value or none at all, you know why you're not feeling great most of the time and what you could do about it. Living our values is what gives us meaning, satisfaction, and joy. Not living our values makes us feel useless, empty, and unhappy. And living in opposition to our values creates more guilt and shame.

WORKSHEET 8.2. Activity Tracking

Today's date:

Time	Actions and activities	Values lived

TABLE 8.1. Duri's Activity Tracking

Today's date: Sunday, December 11, 2022

Time	Actions and activities	Values lived
11 a.m.–12 p.m.	Woke up, scrolled through social media apps in bed, had coffee	Being playful and appreciating humor
12 p.m.–1 p.m.	Scrolled through social media apps in bed	Being playful and appreciating humor
1 p.m.–2 p.m.	Watched videos on phone in bed	Being playful and appreciating humor
. . .	. . .	. . .
4 p.m.–5 p.m.	Ate chips and quick pre-packaged food, started drinking wine; did not answer text or phone call from friend	
5 p.m.–6 p.m.	Looked through to-do list and completed one thing on it: paid rent; continued drinking wine	Being responsible and accountable
6 p.m.–1 a.m.	Played video games and ate snacks, had fast-food delivered; continued drinking wine (finished bottle and started new one)	Being playful and appreciating humor Maintaining mental well-being
1 a.m.–2 a.m.	Passed out without completing hygiene routine	

Duri directly observed these effects when they started tracking their daily activities. They noticed they tended to only live in the service of one value: being playful and appreciating humor. They also initially thought that focusing on doing things that made them laugh was in the service of their mental health. However, the more they checked in with themself, the more they realized they engaged in these behaviors to distract themself and avoid experiencing negative emotions, which resulted in them avoiding doing anything that had real meaning for them. They did have pleasant feelings while watching funny videos or playing games, but these were short-lived. They also noticed that in the long run, they continued to experience negative emotions and self-judgments, which got worse over time. Duri felt empty, listless, and increasingly guilty for not doing things they knew they needed to do, making them want to escape into their distractions even more.

If you find out through this exercise that you are living several different values throughout the day, that's great. Keep it up and see if there are any others you want to move toward also. If you find you are not living your values, that's good to know, too, because once you become aware of that, you make changes to live according to your values more. Even adding one thing per day that aligns with one value can make a difference. And each value-based behavior you add makes it easier to add the next one. Remember the habit-building tips in the Set Yourself Up for Success section of the Introduction? You can review those now to help you add more value-based activities to your life.

WRITING EXERCISE: INCLUDE MORE VALUE-BASED ACTIVITIES IN YOUR SCHEDULE

Find times in your schedule when you could incorporate more of your values into your day. Go over your values on Worksheet 8.1 and identify important ones that are not yet well represented in your schedule. Start by selecting at least one day this week when you want to add at least one more activity that aligns with one of your values. Use Worksheet 8.3 to do this. Pick one small thing you could do that would be in the service of a value you have been neglecting and add it to your schedule for one day this week. For example, is there someone you could call on the phone or spend time with? Do you want to spend 15 minutes looking for a class in an area of interest that you could take? Can you take 30 minutes to go food shopping to buy a few fresh vegetables and fruit that you can include in one meal per day for the week? Could you take a 15-minute walk during lunch?

Add more value-driven activities on more days at the rate that is doable for you. Download extra copies of Worksheet 8.3 at https://www.apa.org/pubs/books/transform-your-guilt-shame (see the Resources tab) as needed.

FOCUS ON THE JOURNEY, NOT THE DESTINATION

An important thing to keep in mind here is that a value is not an outcome. It is not a destination that you get to. It is more like a direction. It's your compass. You can choose to move in the direction of a value or not. But it doesn't change the fact that your value is still in the same direction, and you can choose to move in that direction at any given moment, regardless of what direction you were going in the last moment (or even the last several years, as the case may be).

You will see what I mean in the next example of an activity tracking sheet. This one is typical of clients I have worked with after they have chosen to be more intentional about living their values and have incorporated a bit more into their day each week for a couple of months. Table 8.2 shows what one of Maxwell's tracking sheets looked like 2 months after having interrupted his NAGS cycle.

WORKSHEET 8.3. Planned Schedule to Intentionally Live More Values

Date:

Time	Actions and activities	Values lived

TABLE 8.2. **Maxwell's Activity Tracking**

Today's date: Friday, June 16, 2023

Time	Actions and activities	Values lived
8 a.m.–9 a.m.	Woke up, did morning hygiene routine, had coffee and breakfast, responded to a couple of personal texts and emails	Maintaining energy and well-being Connecting with important others Having compassion and kindness
9 a.m.–10 a.m.	Responded to work emails	Being responsible and accountable
10 a.m.–11 a.m.	Met with supervisor to advocate for team regarding pay concerns	Connecting Having integrity Having courage Treating others fairly and equitably
. . .	. . .	. . .
8 p.m.–10 p.m.	Watched a movie with son— let him pick it	Being playful and appreciating humor Spending quality time with loved ones Maintaining mental well-being

(continues)

TABLE 8.2. Maxwell's Activity Tracking (*Continued*)

Time	Actions and activities	Values lived
10 p.m.–11 p.m.	Reached out to one person I haven't talked to in a long time	Connecting with important others Having compassion and kindness Being responsible and accountable
11 p.m.–12 a.m.	Loaded dishwasher and tidied up a bit, did night-time hygiene routine, went to bed	Being responsible and accountable Maintaining energy and well-being Being a good role model for kids

Can you see that nowhere on this tracking sheet is there any mention of outcomes? Maxwell scheduled and held a meeting to advocate for his team at work. He might have wanted to achieve a certain outcome (e.g., his employer agreeing to pay everyone more), but he lived according to his values regardless of the outcome. And he reaped the benefits of doing so by feeling good about making the effort and doing something meaningful. It's good that the positive effects of living our values are not dependent on the outcome because outcomes are often largely out of our hands. What is in our control is what we do. What we do might influence how things turn out to a certain extent. But too many other factors also play a role in the outcome, so it can never be 100% under our control. The good news is that living our values and not the outcomes of living those values is what brings meaning to our lives.

This doesn't mean you can't have goals or ambitions supporting your values, though. In fact, having goals can be helpful. They can help us engage in value-based activities. For example, while confronting and challenging his guilt and shame, **Felipe** realized that social justice and equity were important values for him. He set many goals related to these values, including a big one of implementing a restorative justice program at work. With this goal in mind, he started making lists of all the things he could do to achieve that goal and added some of these to his day planner. At first, he set aside 30 minutes 3 evenings per week to research and learn all about restorative justice programs. He then set out to find training in restorative justice practices. After he found out how much the training would cost, Felipe added budget-related activities to his schedule. This led him to make changes to his spending. For example, he added 30 minutes to his morning routine so that he could have coffee and breakfast at home instead of going to his regular breakfast spot every morning. He also started asking for additional shifts at work and asked for a raise.

At face value, some of these actions don't seem to be examples of Felipe living his value of "social justice." But they are all moving him toward goals that align with his values. As a result, Felipe found that engaging in these activities made him feel good about himself, his place in the world, and the future. This doesn't mean that he never again felt any negative emotions. Sometimes, he wished he could be eating out instead of making himself a more affordable meal. And there were times when he was upset by a difficult client at work and wished he could be enjoying time off at home instead of having taken on an additional shift. But he was willing to experience these negative emotions because (a) he had learned that he could tolerate these feelings and not have to do anything to get rid of them, (b) he had learned how not to reinforce the feelings by laying negative interpretations on them, and (c) he found that he still felt better overall in the long run by choosing to live his values, even if in the moment it didn't feel pleasant.

CONCLUSION

In the short term, living our values is more difficult and requires more effort than not living our values. But it's well worth the effort because it brings us our sense of meaning, fulfillment, and wellness in the long run. I hope you will give yourself this chance to enjoy these benefits too. It is within your power to use guilt and shame constructively to help you decide how you want to live. And you can choose to do this at any time, regardless of how you have been living up to that point.

WASH, RINSE, REPEAT

I hope you have found this book a valuable and helpful resource and will continue to use it as needed. As I mentioned throughout the book, it may be helpful for you to go back and work with some of your piles of nonadaptive guilt and shame (NAGS) thoughts a few more times before you can challenge them effectively and come up with more accurate and helpful perspectives. Sometimes, our beliefs get ingrained, and like tough stains, we need to wash, rinse, and repeat a few times before they dissolve. Some stains need to soak for a while. Similarly, you can just sit for a bit with all you have learned and realized before coming back to work through some of the steps again.

Whatever the case, please first take stock of what you have done and congratulate yourself. Do this even if you started the process but did not finish working through some of the steps or if you just did a quick read through to see what you could expect. Familiarizing yourself with the process is an important start, and even that probably wasn't easy. Reading this material may have elicited strong negative emotions, and your mind may have tried convincing you of harsh and unhelpful conclusions. Therefore, we can expect strong urges to avoid when confronting our guilt and shame. Under these circumstances, whatever you got through is commendable. So go ahead and reward yourself. And keep rewarding yourself each time you work through another step or go back to rework a step to continue challenging a particularly ingrained NAGS thought.

Another common experience in this process is that getting the reins of your life back is exciting and liberating, but it can also be scary. Anything new can feel scary, even if we know it's for the better. But, as you probably now know, our feelings don't provide us with 100% of the facts. You can remind yourself that just because something is scary doesn't mean it's dangerous or bad. Whenever we do something new, we experience some anxiety because we are not sure what the outcome will be. The anxiety compels us to think about and plan for different possible outcomes, and once we've done that, we can let the anxiety go. It has served its purpose.

It's also important to be aware that just because you have learned new ways of being doesn't mean you will never revert to old habits. You may have regained the reins, but life is not a smooth road. It's bumpy and, sometimes, we get thrown off course. Know that your compass is always there, and you can find your way back on course. And know that you have resources to help you get back on course. You can return to this book whenever you need a reminder of how to stop and get out of a NAGS cycle.

Finally, I do not assume that this book will provide everyone with everything they need to unburden themselves from problematic guilt and shame, use guilt and shame proactively, and get in touch with their values and live according to them. Many circumstances and conditions make going through the steps in this book more challenging, and some people may need to work with a therapist to do so and to address other problems they may be facing. Don't hesitate to access such services. You deserve it, even if you don't yet believe it. Refer to Appendix B for tips on finding quality resources and services.

Whatever you do, keep reminding yourself you have choices and can grab the reins and choose your direction. At any given moment, you can choose to evaluate your thoughts before believing them and keep moving in the direction of your values.

APPENDIX A

WORKSHEETS

Extra copies are available to download at https://www.apa.org/pubs/books/transform-your-guilt-shame (see the Resources tab).

WORKSHEET 2.1. Play-by-Play of the Trauma or Adverse Event

Write about the trauma or adverse event. Write down everything you can recall about the series of events and your thoughts, feelings, and behaviors leading up to, during, and immediately following the adverse event.

WORKSHEET 2.2. Guilt and Shame Thoughts

Write down all thoughts that come up that make you feel guilt or shame when you think about the trauma or adversity you experienced. You will need to return to this worksheet a few times, so you might want to place a bookmark here or fold over the corner of this page so that you can quickly find it.

WORKSHEET 3.1. New, More Accurate, and Helpful Thoughts

Each time you check and challenge one of your guilt and shame thoughts, write your new, more helpful conclusions that are based on the facts on this worksheet. This is where you will collect all your new, more accurate conclusions that you will come to by completing the exercises in the book. You could place a bookmark here or fold over the corner of this page so you can quickly find it and return to it. If you end up printing extra copies of it (which you can do from https://www.apa.org/pubs/books/transform-your-guilt-shame; see the Resources tab), you can tuck them in here to keep all your new, more accurate, and helpful thoughts in one place.

WORKSHEET 4.1. Justification Analysis

1. Write down the possible options you had at the time.
2. Cross out any option that was not available to you because you did not think about it at the time or you did not have the necessary information, skills, or resources to act on it.
3. List the pros and cons you considered at the time.
4. Find the option that had the most compelling pros and least impactful cons. That was your best, most justifiable option.

	Options	Pros	Cons
A			
B			
C			
D			
E			
F			

WORKSHEET 5.1. Responsibility Analysis

1. Write down all the "dominos" that were involved—all the things that contributed to the bad outcome. This includes any circumstances that you had no control over, as well as things you did have control over. Be sure to include the actions of other people, especially the perpetrator, if there is one!
2. Assign responsibility percentages to each contributing factor (without worrying about the math).
3. Total up all your percentages and write this down in the space provided at the bottom of the Assigned % column.
4. Recalculate the relative contribution of each entry in the table by dividing the percentage you assigned it by the total percentage and write these in the right column.

Factors contributing to the situation	Assigned %	Relative %
Total		

Write down everything that contributed to your actions, even the small things. Answer the following questions to get you started.

- Was there a series of events that led to your actions?
- Might you have thought, felt, or acted differently if you had different past experiences?
- Might you have thought, felt, or acted differently if the environment had been different?
- Was your fight–flight–freeze response activated?
- Was avoidance or dissociation activated?
- Did you have any alcohol, street drugs, or over-the-counter or pre-scribed medication in your system that might have influenced your behavior? If so, what led you to take the substance? Were you trying to ease some physical or emotional pain? Were you addicted?
- Did your body respond reflexively to unwanted touching or experiences?

Factors contributing to my thoughts, feelings, and behaviors

WORKSHEET 8.1. My Values

Write down any values that seem important to you for each domain of your life.

Family

Romance

Friendships

Work

Education

Recreation

Mental health

WORKSHEET 8.1. My Values (*Continued*)

Physical health

Finance

Religious or spiritual

Community

Other:

Other:

Other:

WORKSHEET 8.2. Activity Tracking

Today's date:

Time	Actions and activities	Values lived

WORKSHEET 8.3. Planned Schedule to Intentionally Live More Values

Date:

Time	Actions and activities	Values lived

APPENDIX B

RESOURCES

Anyone who has ever conducted an online search or browsed the shelves of a brick-and-mortar bookstore or library in search of a self-help book can attest to how overwhelming that can be. It can be difficult even to know how to start looking. And once you find a few options, how do you know which one will be most helpful? The following is some information that can help you identify some good options.

First, keep in mind that what may have worked well for your hairdresser's neighbor's parent's best friend or even your best friend may not work the same for you. That's because it's not usually possible to know what contributed to one individual recovering from a condition. They may be doing many other things at the same time (some of which they may not be aware of) that contributed to their getting better. As a result, there are many strategies people swear by that were just coincidences. We attribute improvement to something we did just before or when we started feeling better. For example, one of my clients experienced a reduction in their depression when they started taking a vitamin supplement, so they believed this supplement to be a cure for depression, and they joined the company as a sales rep for many months with a mission to get the product into as many hands as possible. The depression returned, and during therapy, they identified other things that could have also helped lift them out of their depression at the time. They were also going for walks daily with their neighbor, work was going well, they were planning a fun trip, and so forth. It's impossible to know what contributed to one individual recovering from a condition unless it's replicated and tested in a controlled way so we can rule out other possible explanations for the improvement. That way, we can identify the active ingredient in the positive changes. That's what scientific studies help us do.

Your best bet is to first try something that was effective in controlled studies. The following organizations provide information about treatments that are effective in treating many different mental health conditions, including posttraumatic stress disorder, major depression, bipolar (previously known as manic depression or mania), generalized anxiety disorder, social anxiety, phobias (e.g., exaggerated fear of spiders, snakes, outdoors, small spaces), panic (or anxiety attacks), obsessive-compulsive disorder, substance use disorder (which can also be called alcohol or drug abuse, dependence, or addiction), schizophrenia (psychosis), borderline personality disorder, and dissociative identity disorder:

- American Psychiatric Association (https://www.psychiatryonline.org)
- American Psychological Association (https://www.apa.org)
- Anxiety & Depression Association of America (https://www.aada.org)
- Australian Government Department of Health and Aged Care (https://www.health.gov.au)
- Australian Psychological Society (https://www.psychology.org.au)
- Canadian Mental Health Association (https://www.cmha.ca)
- Canadian Psychological Association (https://www.cpa.ca)

- International Society for the Study of Trauma and Dissociation (https://www.isst-d.org)
- International Society for Traumatic Stress Studies (https://www.istss.org)
- National Association of Addiction Treatment Providers (https://www.naatp.org)
- National Institute on Alcohol Abuse and Alcoholism (https://www.niaaa.nih.gov)
- National Institute of Mental Health (https://www.nimh.nih.gov)
- Substance Abuse and Mental Health Services Administration (https://www.samhsa.gov)
- United Kingdom National Health Service (https://www.nhs.uk)
- World Health Organization (https://www.who.int)

As you will see, there is more than one effective treatment for many conditions. Some of the resource sites have treatment decisional aids you can use to help you decide which one to pursue. Because there are no hard or fast rules about which will work best with whom, your decision will largely be a matter of choice and/or availability. Some therapists are trained in more than one effective treatment and can help you decide which one is the best fit for you. But many will specialize in just one type. Either way, you should feel confident that you are starting with a therapy that is effective for most people.

The other important thing to keep in mind is that just because a provider or their website says they use cognitive behavior therapy, it doesn't necessarily mean they do or that they administer the treatment in the way that is effective in the research studies. You will want to ask your provider what kind of treatment they provide and why, what kind of training they received, and what their effectiveness rates are at implementing these treatments. If they have difficulty or get defensive discussing these things with you or answering all your questions, it's a red flag that they may not provide scientifically backed effective treatments. Another red flag is if they tell you that all their clients have recovered 100% from the conditions for which they were treated. As of yet, there are no mental health treatments that are 100% effective for everyone.

Finally, a good treatment provider will first conduct a comprehensive assessment to make sure they understand your most impactful symptoms and the contexts in which they arise and produce the most problems for you. This is necessary for developing a good understanding of what is going on, assigning accurate diagnoses, and developing a treatment plan that includes the most effective therapy best suited to meet your therapy goals in your current context.

APPENDIX C

SCIENTIFIC EVIDENCE

The following are references for all the scientific evidence supporting the information and strategies presented in the book. Readers
will find most of the references for the scientific evidence on which
this book is based in the trauma informed guilt reduction (TrIGR)
therapy manual:

Norman, S., Allard, C., Browne, K., Capone, C., Davis, B., & Kubany, E.
(2019). *Trauma informed guilt reduction therapy: Treating guilt and
shame resulting from trauma and moral injury.* Academic Press.

The rest of the references provide additional scientific and theoretical support for the TrIGR approach that emerged after we finished
writing the manual and scientific evidence for some of the additional
self-help focused tips I provide in this book.

Affleck, W., Thamotharampillai, U., Jeyakumar, J., & Whitley, R. (2018).
"If one does not fulfil his duties, he must not be a man": Masculinity, mental health and resilience amongst Sri Lankan Tamil refugee
men in Canada. *Culture, Medicine, and Psychiatry, 42*(4), 840–861.
https://doi.org/10.1007/s11013-018-9592-9

Allard, C. B., Norman, S. B., Straus, E., Kim, H. M., Stein, M. B., Simon,
N. M., & Rauch, S. A. M. (2021). Reductions in guilt cognitions following prolonged exposure and/or sertraline predict subsequent improve-
ments in PTSD and depression. *Journal of Behavior Therapy and*

Experimental Psychiatry, 73, Article 101666. https://doi.org/10.1016/j.jbtep.2021.101666

Allard, C. B., Norman, S. B., Thorp, S. R., Browne, K. C., & Stein, M. B. (2018). Mid-treatment reduction in trauma-related guilt predicts PTSD and functioning following cognitive trauma therapy for survivors of intimate partner violence. *Journal of Interpersonal Violence, 33*(23), 3610–3629. https://doi.org/10.1177/0886260516636068

Anderson, C. L. (1982). Males as sexual assault victims: Multiple levels of trauma. *Journal of Homosexuality, 7*(2–3), 145–162. https://doi.org/10.1300/J082v07n02_15

Artime, T. M., & Peterson, Z. D. (2015). Feelings of wantedness and consent during nonconsensual sex: Implications for posttraumatic cognitions. *Psychological Trauma: Theory, Research, Practice, and Policy, 7*(6), 570–577. https://doi.org/10.1037/tra0000047

Aurora, P., LoSavio, S. T., Kimbrel, N. A., Beckham, J. C., Calhoun, P. S., & Dillon, K. H. (2023). Examining the daily relationship between guilt, shame, and substance use among veterans with psychiatric disorders. *Drug and Alcohol Dependence Reports, 8*, Article 100174. https://doi.org/10.1016/j.dadr.2023.100174

Bomyea, J., & Allard, C. B. (2017). Trauma-related disgust in veterans with interpersonal trauma. *Journal of Traumatic Stress, 30*(2), 149–156. https://doi.org/10.1002/jts.22169

Borges, L. M., Desai, A., Barnes, S. M., & Johnson, J. P. S. (2022). The role of social determinants of health in moral injury: Implications and future directions. *Current Treatment Options in Psychiatry, 9*(3), 202–214. https://doi.org/10.1007/s40501-022-00272-4

Borges, L. M., Holliday, R., Barnes, S. M., Bahraini, N. H., Kinney, A., Forster, J. E., & Brenner, L. A. (2021). A longitudinal analysis of the role of potentially morally injurious events on COVID-19-related psychosocial functioning among healthcare providers. *PLOS ONE, 16*(11), Article e0260033. https://doi.org/10.1371/journal.pone.0260033

Bryan, A. O., Bryan, C. J., Morrow, C. E., Etienne, N., & Ray-Sannerud, B. (2014). Moral injury, suicidal ideation, and suicide attempts in a military sample. *Traumatology, 20*(3), 154–160. https://doi.org/10.1037/h0099852

Bryan, C. J., Griffith, J. E., Pace, B. T., Hinkson, K., Bryan, A. O., Clemans, T. A., & Imel, Z. E. (2015). Combat exposure and risk for suicidal thoughts and behaviors among military personnel and veterans: A systematic review and meta-analysis. *Suicide and Life-Threatening Behavior, 45*(5), 633–649. https://doi.org/10.1111/sltb.12163

Bryant-Davis, T., & Ocampo, C. (2005). Racist incident–based trauma. *The Counseling Psychologist, 33*(4), 479–500. https://doi.org/10.1177/0011000005276465

Bufka, L. (2022, August 8). Why COVID makes so many of us feel guilty. *Scientific American.* https://www.scientificamerican.com/article/why-covid-makes-so-many-of-us-feel-guilty/

Bullock, C. M., & Beckson, M. (2011). Male victims of sexual assault: Phenomenology, psychology, physiology. *Journal of the American Academy of Psychiatry and the Law, 39*(2), 197–205.

Bunderson, K. (2020). *Female sexual arousal during rape: Implications on seeking treatment, blame, and the emotional experience* [Unpublished doctoral dissertation]. Alliant International University.

Burback, L., Brémault-Phillips, S., Nijdam, M. J., McFarlane, A., & Vermetten, E. (2024). Treatment of posttraumatic stress disorder: A state-of-the-art review. *Current Neuropharmacology, 22*(4), 557–635. https://doi.org/10.2174/1570159X21666230428091433

Capone, C., Norman, S. B., Haller, M., Davis, B., Shea, M. T., Browne, K., Lang, A. J., Schnurr, P. P., Golshan, S., Afari, N., Pittman, J., Allard, C. B., & Westendorf, L. (2021). Trauma informed guilt reduction (TrIGR) therapy for guilt, shame, and moral injury resulting from trauma: Rationale, design, and methodology of a two-site randomized controlled trial. *Contemporary Clinical Trials, 101,* Article 106251. https://doi.org/10.1016/j.cct.2020.106251

Carroll, K. K., Lofgreen, A. M., Weaver, D. C., Held, P., Klassen, B. J., Smith, D. L., Karnik, N. S., Pollack, M. H., & Zalta, A. K. (2018). Negative posttraumatic cognitions among military sexual trauma survivors. *Journal of Affective Disorders, 238,* 88–93. https://doi.org/10.1016/j.jad.2018.05.024

Cavalera, C. (2020, November 2). COVID-19 psychological implications: The role of shame and guilt. *Frontiers in Psychology, 11,* Article 571828. https://doi.org/10.3389/fpsyg.2020.571828

Cénat, J. M. (2023). Complex racial trauma: Evidence, theory, assessment, and treatment. *Perspectives on Psychological Science, 18*(3), 675–687. https://doi.org/10.1177/17456916221120428

Chamberlin, E. S., Usset, T. J., Fantus, S., Kondrath, S. R., Butler, M., Weber, M. C., & Wilson, M. A. (2023). Moral injury in healthcare: Adapting the Building Spiritual Strength (BSS) intervention to Health and Strength (HAS) for civilian and military healthcare workers. *Current Treatment Options in Psychiatry, 10*(3), 234–247. https://doi.org/10.1007/s40501-023-00294-6

Chou, P.-H., Wang, S.-C., Wu, C.-S., & Ito, M. (2023, March 27). Trauma-related guilt as a mediator between post-traumatic stress disorder and suicidal ideation. *Frontiers in Psychiatry, 14,* Article 1131733. https://doi.org/10.3389/fpsyt.2023.1131733

Clausen, L. (2022). Diabolical perspectives on healthy morality in times of COVID-19. *Kybernetes, 51*(5), 1692–1709. https://doi.org/10.1108/K-02-2021-0155

Cole, A. C., Smirnova, M. O., Yang, Y., & Lancaster, C. L. (2023). Longitudinal associations between moral injury perceptions and mental health among healthcare workers during the pandemic. *Psychological Trauma: Theory, Research, Practice, and Policy.* Advance online publication. https://doi.org/10.1037/tra0001594

Comas-Díaz, L. (2016). Racial trauma recovery: A race-informed therapeutic approach to racial wounds. In A. N. Alvarez, C. T. H. Liang, & H. A. Neville (Eds.), *The cost of racism for people of color: Contextualizing experiences of discrimination* (pp. 249–272). American Psychological Association. https://doi.org/10.1037/14852-012

Davis, J. P., Canning, L., Saba, S. K., Bravo, A. J., Amone-P'Olak, K., Sedano, A., Tran, D., Castro, C., & Pedersen, E. R. (2023). Associations between trauma-related guilt, symptoms of posttraumatic stress disorder, and problematic alcohol use. *Psychiatry Research, 326,* Article 115350. https://doi.org/10.1016/j.psychres.2023.115350

Ducharlet, K., Trivedi, M., Gelfand, S. L., Liew, H., McMahon, L. P., Ashuntantang, G., Brennan, F., Brown, M., & Martin, D. E. (2021). Moral distress and moral injury in nephrology during the COVID-19 pandemic. *Seminars in Nephrology, 41*(3), 253–261. https://doi.org/10.1016/j.semnephrol.2021.05.006

Efthim, P. W., Kenny, M. E., & Mahalik, J. R. (2001). Gender role stress in relation to shame, guilt, and externalization. *Journal of Counseling & Development, 79*(4), 430–438. https://doi.org/10.1002/j.1556-6676.2001.tb01990.x

Elder, W., Domino, J., Mata-Galán, E., & Kilmartin, C. (2017). Masculinity as an avoidance symptom of posttraumatic stress. *Psychology of Men & Masculinity, 18*(3), 198–207. https://doi.org/10.1037/men0000123

Evans, S. Y., Bell, K., & Burton, N. K. (Eds.). (2017). *Black women's mental health: Balancing strength and vulnerability.* SUNY Press. https://doi.org/10.1353/book52371

Fischer, I. C., Norman, S. B., Feder, A., Feingold, J. H., Peccoralo, L., Ripp, J., & Pietrzak, R. H. (2022). Downstream consequences of moral distress in COVID-19 frontline healthcare workers: Longitudinal associations with moral injury-related guilt. *General Hospital Psychiatry, 79,* 158–161. https://doi.org/10.1016/j.genhosppsych.2022.11.003

Flynn, A. J., Puhalla, A., & Vaught, A. (2023). The role of shame and trauma type on posttraumatic stress disorder and depression severity in a treatment-seeking veteran population. *Psychological Trauma: Theory, Research, Practice, and Policy.* Advance online publication. https://doi.org/10.1037/tra0001495

Fox, J., & Pease, B. (2012). Military deployment, masculinity and trauma: Reviewing the connections. *The Journal of Men's Studies, 20*(1), 16–31. https://doi.org/10.3149/jms.2001.16

French, L., Hanna, P., & Huckle, C. (2022). "If I die, they do not care": U.K. National Health Service staff experiences of betrayal-based moral injury during COVID-19. *Psychological Trauma: Theory, Research, Practice, and Policy, 14*(3), 516–521. https://doi.org/10.1037/tra0001134

Fulton, T., Lathan, E. C., Karkare, M. C., Guelfo, A., Eghbalzad, L., Ahluwalia, V., Ely, T. D., Turner, J. A., Turner, M. D., Currier, J. M., Mekawi, Y., & Fani, N. (2024). Civilian moral injury and amygdala functional connectivity during attention to threat. *Biological Psychiatry: Cognitive Neuroscience and Neuroimaging, 9*(1), 112–120. https://doi.org/10.1016/j.bpsc.2023.07.006

Gallagher, A. R., Rickman, S. R. M., & Yalch, M. M. (2023). Influence of maladaptive personality traits on women's posttraumatic cognitions of IPV. *Psychological Trauma: Theory, Research, Practice, and Policy, 15*(1), 73–79. https://doi.org/10.1037/tra0001317

Gámez-Guadix, M., Mateos-Pérez, E., Alcázar, M. A., Martínez-Bacaicoa, J., & Wachs, S. (2023). Stability of the online grooming victimization of minors: Prevalence and association with shame, guilt, and mental health outcomes over one year. *Journal of Adolescence, 95*(8), 1715–1724. https://doi.org/10.1002/jad.12240

Gewirtz-Meydan, A., & Godbout, N. (2023). Between pleasure, guilt, and dissociation: How trauma unfolds in the sexuality of childhood sexual abuse survivors. *Child Abuse & Neglect, 141*, Article 106195. https://doi.org/10.1016/j.chiabu.2023.106195

Gilbert-Ouimet, M., Zahiriharsini, A., Biron, C., Langlois, L., Ménard, C., Lebel, M., Pelletier, J., Duchaine, C., Beaulieu, M., & Truchon, M. (2022). Predict, prevent and manage moral injuries in Canadian frontline healthcare workers and leaders facing the COVID-19 pandemic: Protocol of a mixed methods study. *SSM Mental Health, 2*, Article 100124. https://doi.org/10.1016/j.ssmmh.2022.100124

Giwa, A., Crutchfield, D., Fletcher, D., Gemmill, J., Kindrat, J., Smith, A., & Bayless, P. (2021). Addressing moral injury in emergency medicine. *The Journal of Emergency Medicine, 61*(6), 782–788. https://doi.org/10.1016/j.jemermed.2021.07.066

Gorlin, E. I., Békés, V., & Mazer, L. M. (2021). Supporting healthcare workers involved in medical errors: From "second victims" to "resilient warriors." *BMJ, 375*(2745). Advance online publication. https://doi.org/10.1136/bmj.n2745

Grady, C. (2022). The emotional and moral remnants of COVID-19: Burnout, moral distress, and mental health concerns. In C. M. Ulrich & C. Grady (Eds.), *Nurses and COVID-19: Ethical considerations in pandemic care* (pp. 53–62). Springer. https://doi.org/10.1007/978-3-030-82113-5_5

Haller, M., Norman, S. B., Davis, B. C., Capone, C., Browne, K., & Allard, C. B. (2020). A model for treating COVID-19-related guilt, shame, and moral injury. *Psychological Trauma: Theory, Research, Practice, and Policy, 12*(S1), S174–S176. https://doi.org/10.1037/tra0000742

Hamama, L., & Levin-Dagan, N. (2022). People who contracted COVID-19: The mediating role of shame and guilt in the link between threatening illness perception and mental health measures. *Anxiety, Stress & Coping, 35*(1), 72–85. https://doi.org/10.1080/10615806.2021.1964073

Harris-Perry, M. V. (2011). *Sister citizen: Shame, stereotypes, and Black women in America.* Yale University Press.

Hegarty, S., Lamb, D., Stevelink, S. A. M., Bhundia, R., Raine, R., Doherty, M. J., Scott, H. R., Marie Rafferty, A., Williamson, V., Dorrington, S., Hotopf, M., Razavi, R., Greenberg, N., & Wessely, S. (2022). 'It hurts your heart': Frontline healthcare worker experiences of moral injury during the COVID-19 pandemic. *European Journal of Psychotraumatology, 13*(2), Article 2128028. https://doi.org/10.1080/20008066.2022.2128028

Herman, J. L. (2011). Posttraumatic stress disorder as a shame disorder. In R. L. Dearing & J. P. Tangney (Eds.), *Shame in the therapy hour* (pp. 261–275). American Psychological Association. https://doi.org/10.1037/12326-011

Hollis, J., Hanna, P., & Perman, G. (2023). Recontextualising moral injury among military veterans: An integrative theoretical review. *Journal of Community & Applied Social Psychology, 33*(1), 85–101. https://doi.org/10.1002/casp.2643

Houle, S. A., & Ashbaugh, A. R. (2023, August 1). Predictors of negative moral appraisals and their association with symptoms of posttraumatic stress and depression in the context of COVID-19 related stressors. *Stress and Health.* Advance online publication. https://doi.org/10.1002/smi.3296

Howe, E. G. (2020). Optimal approaches to pregnant women with COVID-19. *International Journal of Pregnancy & Child Birth, 6*(4), 81–84. https://doi.org/10.15406/ipcb.2020.06.00202

Irwin, K. E., & Loscalzo, M. L. (2020). Witnessing unnecessary suffering: A call for action and policy change to increase access to psychooncology care. *Psycho-Oncology, 29*(12), 1977–1981. https://doi.org/10.1002/pon.5599

Jamieson, N., Maple, M., Ratnarajah, D., & Usher, K. (2020). Military moral injury: A concept analysis. *International Journal of Mental Health Nursing, 29*(6), 1049–1066. https://doi.org/10.1111/inm.12792

Jamieson, N., Usher, K., Ratnarajah, D., & Maple, M. (2021). Walking forwards with moral injury: Narratives from ex-serving Australian Defence Force members. *Journal of Veterans Studies, 7*(1), 174–185. https://doi.org/10.21061/jvs.v7i1.214

Jansson, P. M. (2019). Exploring pathways related to men's violence: A qualitative exploration of the relationship between violent men's violence and their masculinities, childhood, and emotions. *Deviant Behavior, 40*(10), 1171–1186. https://doi.org/10.1080/01639625.2018.1472929

Juan, M. J. D., Nunnink, S. E., Butler, E. O., & Allard, C. B. (2017). Gender role stress mediates depression among veteran men with military sexual trauma. *Psychology of Men & Masculinity, 18*(3), 243–250. https://doi.org/10.1037/men0000120

Kalmbach, K., Basinger, E., Bayles, B., Schmitt, R., Nunez, V., Moore, B., & Tedeschi, R. (2023). Moral injury in post-9/11 combat-experienced military veterans: A qualitative thematic analysis. *Psychological Services*. Advance online publication. https://doi.org/10.1037/ser0000792

Kealy, D., Treeby, M. S., & Rice, S. M. (2021). Shame, guilt, and suicidal thoughts: The interaction matters. *British Journal of Clinical Psychology, 60*(3), 414–423. https://doi.org/10.1111/bjc.12291

Khan, A. J., Griffin, B. J., & Maguen, S. (2023). A review of research on moral injury and suicide risk. *Current Treatment Options in Psychiatry, 10*(3), 259–287. https://doi.org/10.1007/s40501-023-00293-7

Khan, F. A. (2021). Anesthesiologists' occupational wellbeing and support during COVID-19 pandemic. *Anaesthesia, Pain & Intensive Care, 25*(2), 122–125. https://doi.org/10.35975/apic.v25i2.1459

Kip, A., Diele, J., Holling, H., & Morina, N. (2022). The relationship of trauma-related guilt with PTSD symptoms in adult trauma survivors: A meta-analysis. *Psychological Medicine, 52*(12), 2201–2211. https://doi.org/10.1017/S0033291722001866

Konopasky, A., Bunin, J. L., & Varpio, L. (2022). The philosophy of agency: Agency as a protective mechanism against clinical trainees' moral injury. In M. E. L. Brown, M. Veen, & G. M. Finn (Eds.), *Applied philosophy for health professions education: A journey towards mutual understanding* (pp. 157–171). Springer. https://doi.org/10.1007/978-981-19-1512-3_11

Kooistra, M. J., Hoeboer, C. M., Oprel, D. A. C., Schoorl, M., van der Does, W., Ter Heide, J. J., van Minnen, A., & de Kleine, R. A. (2023). Changes in trauma-related cognitions predict subsequent symptom improvement during prolonged exposure in patients with childhood abuse-related PTSD. *Behaviour Research and Therapy, 163*, Article 104284. https://doi.org/10.1016/j.brat.2023.104284

Kuck, S., Arntz, A., Rameckers, S. A., Lee, C. W., Boterhoven de Haan, K. L., Fassbinder, E., & Morina, N. (2023). Intraindividual variability and emotional change as predictors of sudden gains in imagery rescripting and EMDR for PTSD in adult survivors of childhood abuse.

Clinical Psychology & Psychotherapy, 30(5), 1029–1046. https:// doi.org/10.1002/cpp.2855

Kulla, P., Braun, T., Reichenberger, T., & Kruse, J. (2023). Researching shame, dissociation, and their relationship using latent change modeling. *Journal of Experimental Psychopathology, 14*(2). Advance online publication. https://doi.org/10.1177/20438087231162756

Lamiani, G., Borghi, L., Poli, S., Razzini, K., Colosio, C., & Vegni, E. (2021). Hospital employees' well-being six months after the COVID-19 outbreak: Results from a psychological screening program in Italy. *International Journal of Environmental Research and Public Health, 18*(11), Article 5649. https://doi.org/10.3390/ijerph18115649

Lathan, E. C., Powers, A., Kottakis, A., Guelfo, A., Siegle, G. J., Turner, J. A., Turner, M. D., Yakkanti, V., Jain, J., Mekawi, Y., Teer, A. P., Currier, J. M., & Fani, N. (2023). Civilian moral injury: Associations with trauma type and high-frequency heart rate variability in two trauma-exposed community-based samples. *Psychological Medicine, 53*(11), 5136–5145. https://doi.org/10.1017/S003329172200215X

Lee, S. A., Neimeyer, R. A., Mancini, V. O., & Breen, L. J. (2022). Unfinished business and self-blaming emotions among those bereaved by a COVID-19 death. *Death Studies, 46*(6), 1297–1306. https://doi.org/ 10.1080/07481187.2022.2067640

Levin, R. J., & van Berlo, W. (2004). Sexual arousal and orgasm in subjects who experience forced or non-consensual sexual stimulation—A review. *Journal of Clinical Forensic Medicine, 11*(2), 82–88. https://doi.org/ 10.1016/j.jcfm.2003.10.008

Levy, A., & Gross, M. (2023). *How moral injury and combat trauma drive political activism and societal reintegration among Israeli veterans.* https://doi.org/10.13140/RG.2.2.20962.91845

Liang, T., Kaka Mirza, H., Malakoutikhah, A., Dehghan, M., Mokhtarabadi, S., Behzadi Fard, S., & Al-Amer, R. (2023). Moral injury and its correlates among Iranian nurses in the second year of the COVID-19 pandemic: A multicenter cross-sectional study. *Journal of Religion and Health, 62*(6), 3979–3994. https://doi.org/10.1007/ s10943-023-01938-w

Lindberg, F. H., & Distad, L. J. (1985). Post-traumatic stress disorders in women who experienced childhood incest. *Child Abuse & Neglect, 9*(3), 329–334. https://doi.org/10.1016/0145-2134(85)90028-6

Linsley, P. (2021). Trauma informed guilt reduction therapy: Treating guilt and shame resulting from trauma and moral injury. *Journal of Mental Health, 30*(1), 134. https://doi.org/10.1080/09638237.2021.1875425

Maguen, S., & Griffin, B. J. (2022, April 14). Research gaps and recommendations to guide research on assessment, prevention, and treatment of moral injury among healthcare workers. *Frontiers in Psychiatry, 13,* Article 874729. https://doi.org/10.3389/fpsyt.2022.874729

McCann, J. P., Tipsword, J. M., Brake, C. A., & Badour, C. L. (2023). Trauma-related shame and guilt as prospective predictors of daily mental contamination and PTSD symptoms in survivors of sexual trauma. *Journal of Interpersonal Violence, 38*(19–20), 11117–11137. https://doi.org/10.1177/08862605231179721

McCue, M. L., Fisher, A. N., Johnson, K. R., Allard, C. B., & Tiet, Q. Q. (2022). Veteran suicide exposure: Associations with guilt, PTSD, and suicidality. *Journal of Veterans Studies, 8*(3), 1–12. https://doi.org/10.21061/jvs.v8i3.317

McCue, M. L., Fisher, A. N., Johnson, K. R., Bariani, A., Cabral, M. M., Edmonds, S., Allard, C. B., & Tiet, Q. Q. (2021). Exposure to civilian casualties is related to guilt and suicidality in post 9/11 veterans of Iraq and Afghanistan. *Military Behavioral Health, 9*(1), 110–117. https://doi.org/10.1080/21635781.2021.1904065

McDaniel, J. T., Redner, R., Jayawardene, W., Haun, J., Clapp, J., Che, D., Renzaglia, K., & Abou-Jabal, D. (2023). Moral injury is a risk factor for substance use and suicidality among US Military veterans with and without traumatic brain injury. *Journal of Religion and Health, 62*(6), 3926–3941. https://doi.org/10.1007/s10943-023-01905-5

McDermott, R. C., Currier, J. M., Naylor, P. D., & Kuhlman, S. T. W. (2017). Student veterans' self-stigma of seeking help: Contributions of painful self-conscious emotions, traditional masculine norms, and war-zone service. *Psychology of Men & Masculinity, 18*(3), 226–237. https://doi.org/10.1037/men0000117

Meade, E. A., Smith, D. L., Montes, M., Norman, S. B., & Held, P. (2022). Changes in guilt cognitions in intensive PTSD treatment among veterans who experienced military sexual trauma or combat trauma. *Journal of Anxiety Disorders, 90,* Article 102606. https://doi.org/10.1016/j.janxdis.2022.102606

Mensink, B., van Schagen, A., van der Aa, N., & Ter Heide, F. J. J. (2022, July 10). Moral injury in trauma-exposed, treatment-seeking police officers and military veterans: Latent class analysis. *Frontiers in Psychiatry, 13*, Article 904659. https://doi.org/10.3389/fpsyt.2022.904659

Mitchell, D., Hirschman, R., & Nagayama Hall, G. C. (1999). Attributions of victim responsibility, pleasure, and trauma in male rape. *Journal of Sex Research, 36*(4), 369–373. https://doi.org/10.1080/00224499909552009

Mooren, N., Boelen, P. A., & de la Rie, S. M. (2022, September 7). The impact of morally injurious events in a refugee sample: A quantitative and qualitative study. *Frontiers in Psychiatry, 13*, Article 904808. https://doi.org/10.3389/fpsyt.2022.904808

Naismith, I., Ripoll-Nuñez, K., & Henao, G. B. (2022). Depression, anxiety, and posttraumatic stress disorder following intimate partner violence: The role of self-criticism, guilt, and gender beliefs. *Violence Against Women, 30*(3–4), 791–811. https://doi.org/10.1177/10778012221142917

Norman, S. (2022). Trauma-informed guilt reduction therapy: Overview of the treatment and research. *Current Treatment Options in Psychiatry, 9*(3), 115–125. https://doi.org/10.1007/s40501-022-00261-7

Norman, S., Allard, C., Browne, K., Capone, C., Davis, B., & Kubany, E. (2019). *Trauma informed guilt reduction therapy: Treating guilt and shame resulting from trauma and moral injury.* Academic Press.

Norman, S. B., Capone, C., Panza, K. E., Haller, M., Davis, B. C., Schnurr, P. P., Shea, M. T., Browne, K., Norman, G. J., Lang, A. J., Kline, A. C., Golshan, S., Allard, C. B., & Angkaw, A. (2022). A clinical trial comparing trauma-informed guilt reduction therapy (TrIGR), a brief intervention for trauma-related guilt, to supportive care therapy. *Depression and Anxiety, 39*(4), 262–273. https://doi.org/10.1002/da.23244

Norman, S. B., Feingold, J. H., Kaye-Kauderer, H., Kaplan, C. A., Hurtado, A., Kachadourian, L., Feder, A., Murrough, J. W., Charney, D., Southwick, S. M., Ripp, J., Peccoralo, L., & Pietrzak, R. H. (2021). Moral distress in frontline healthcare workers in the initial epicenter of the COVID-19 pandemic in the United States: Relationship to PTSD symptoms, burnout, and psychosocial functioning. *Depression and Anxiety, 38*(10), 1007–1017. https://doi.org/10.1002/da.23205

Norman, S. B., Haller, M., Kim, H. M., Allard, C. B., Porter, K. E., Stein, M. B., Venners, M. R., Authier, C. C., & Rauch, S. A. M. (2018). Trauma related guilt cognitions partially mediate the relationship between PTSD symptom severity and functioning among returning combat veterans. *Journal of Psychiatric Research, 100*, 56–62. https://doi.org/10.1016/j.jpsychires.2018.02.003

Norman, S. B., Nichter, B., Maguen, S., Na, P. J., Schnurr, P. P., & Pietrzak, R. H. (2022). Moral injury among U.S. combat veterans with and without PTSD and depression. *Journal of Psychiatric Research, 154*, 190–197. https://doi.org/10.1016/j.jpsychires.2022.07.033

Norman, S. B., Wilkins, K. C., Myers, U. S., & Allard, C. B. (2014). Trauma informed guilt reduction therapy with combat veterans. *Cognitive and Behavioral Practice, 21*(1), 78–88. https://doi.org/10.1016/j.cbpra.2013.08.001

Oh, H., Lee, D. G., & Cho, H. (2023, September 27). The differential roles of shame and guilt in the relationship between self-discrepancy and psychological maladjustment. *Frontiers in Psychology, 14*, Article 1215177. https://doi.org/10.3389/fpsyg.2023.1215177

Orak, U., Kelton, K., Vaughn, M., Tsai, J., & Pietrzak, R. (2023). Homelessness and contact with the criminal legal system among U.S. combat veterans: An exploration of potential mediating factors. *Criminal Justice and Behavior, 50*(3), 392–409. https://doi.org/10.1177/00938548221140352

Peccoralo, L. A., Pietrzak, R. H., Feingold, J. H., Syed, S., Chan, C. C., Murrough, J. W., Kaplan, C., Verity, J., Feder, A., Charney, D. S., Southwick, S. M., & Ripp, J. A. (2022). A prospective cohort study of the psychological consequences of the COVID-19 pandemic on front-line healthcare workers in New York City. *International Archives of Occupational and Environmental Health, 95*(6), 1279–1291. https://doi.org/10.1007/s00420-022-01832-0

Rameckers, S. A., van Emmerik, A. A. P., Grasman, R. P. P. P., & Arntz, A. (2024). Non-fear emotions in changes in posttraumatic stress disorder symptoms during treatment. *Journal of Behavior Therapy and Experimental Psychiatry*, Article 101954. https://doi.org/10.1016/j.jbtep.2024.101954

Rathgeber, I., Rohrer, B., & Andreatta, P. (2022). Im dienst der gesundheit: Wenn die belastungen in folge des SARS-CoV-2 für das personal zum traumastress werden [In the service of health: When the stress caused by SARS-CoV-2 becomes traumatic stress for staff]. *Procare: das Forbildungsmagazin fur Pflegeberufe, 27*(5), 50–53. https://doi.org/10.1007/s00735-022-1573-0

Rentoul, L., & Appleboom, N. (1997). Understanding the psychological impact of rape and serious sexual assault of men: A literature review. *Journal of Psychiatric and Mental Health Nursing, 4*(4), 267–274. https://doi.org/10.1046/j.1365-2850.1997.00064.x

Resnick, K. S., & Fins, J. J. (2021). Professionalism and resilience after COVID-19. *Academic Psychiatry, 45*(5), 552–556. https://doi.org/10.1007/s40596-021-01416-z

Rodríguez, E. A., Agüero-Flores, M., Landa-Blanco, M., Agurcia, D., & Santos-Midence, C. (2021). Moral injury and light triad traits: Anxiety and depression in health-care personnel during the Coronavirus-2019 pandemic in Honduras. *Hispanic Health Care International, 19*(4), 230–238. https://doi.org/10.1177/15404153211042371

Roth, S., & Newman, E. (1991). The process of coping with sexual trauma. *Journal of Traumatic Stress, 4*(2), 279–297. https://doi.org/10.1002/jts.2490040209

Rudy, J. A., McKernan, S., Kouri, N., & D'Andrea, W. (2022). A meta-analysis of the association between shame and dissociation. *Journal of Traumatic Stress, 35*(5), 1318–1333. https://doi.org/10.1002/jts.22854

Saraiya, T., Badour, C., Jones, A., Jarnecke, A., Brown, D., Flanagan, J., Killeen, T., & Back, S. (2023). The role of posttraumatic guilt and anger in integrated treatment for PTSD and co-occurring substance use disorders among primarily male veterans. *Psychological Trauma: Theory, Research, Practice, and Policy, 15*(8), 1293–1298. https://doi.org/10.1037/tra0001204

Schoenfarber, A., & Langan, S. (2023). Communicable diseases. In M. Hemphill & A. Nathanson (Eds.), *The practice of clinical social work in healthcare* (pp. 63–86). Springer. https://doi.org/10.1007/978-3-031-31650-0_4

Serfioti, D., Murphy, D., Greenberg, N., & Williamson, V. (2022). Effectiveness of treatments for symptoms of post-trauma related guilt, shame and anger in military and civilian populations: A systematic review. *BMJ Military Health*. Advance online publication. https://doi.org/10.1136/military-2022-002155

Shi, C., Ren, Z., Zhao, C., Zhang, T., & Chan, S. H.-W. (2021). Shame, guilt, and posttraumatic stress symptoms: A three-level meta-analysis. *Journal of Anxiety Disorders, 82,* Article 102443. https://doi.org/ 10.1016/j.janxdis.2021.102443

Shields, D. M., Kuhl, D., & Westwood, M. J. (2017). Abject masculinity and the military: Articulating a fulcrum of struggle and change. *Psychology of Men & Masculinity, 18*(3), 215–225. https://doi.org/10.1037/ men0000114

Shin, H. J., & Salter, M. (2022). Betrayed by my body: Survivor experiences of sexual arousal and psychological pleasure during sexual violence. *Journal of Gender-Based Violence, 6*(3), 581–595. https://doi.org/ 10.1332/239868021X16430290699192

Siegel, A., Shaked, E., & Lahav, Y. (2022). A complex relationship: Intimate partner violence, identification with the aggressor, and guilt. *Violence Against Women, 30*(2), 445–459.

Suomi, A., Schofield, T. P., & Butterworth, P. (2020, October 14). Unemployment, employability and COVID19: How the global socioeconomic shock challenged negative perceptions toward the less fortunate in the Australian context. *Frontiers in Psychology, 11,* Article 594837. https://doi.org/10.3389/fpsyg.2020.594837

ter Heide, F. J. J., de Goede, M. L., van Dam, S., & Ekkers, S. (2022, September 1). Development of an online supportive treatment module for moral injury in military veterans and police officers. *Frontiers in Psychiatry, 13,* Article 890858. https://doi.org/10.3389/fpsyt.2022. 890858

ter Heide, J. J., & Olff, M. (2023). Widening the scope: Defining and treating moral injury in diverse populations. *European Journal of Psychotraumatology, 14*(2), Article 2196899. https://doi.org/10.1080/ 20008066.2023.2196899

Tytarenko, T., Vasiutynskyi, V., Hubeladze, I., Chunikhina, S., & Hromova, H. (2023). War-related life-making landscapes: Ukrainian context. *Journal of Loss and Trauma, 29*(2), 154–178. https://doi.org/10.1080/ 15325024.2023.2256219

Van Denend, J., Harris, J. I., Fuehrlein, B., & Edens, E. L. (2022). Moral injury in the context of substance use disorders: A narrative review. *Current Treatment Options in Psychiatry, 9*(4), 321–330. https:// doi.org/10.1007/s40501-022-00280-4

Walker-Barnes, C. (2017). When the bough breaks: The StrongBlackWoman and the embodiment of stress. In S. Y. Evans, K. Bell, & N. K. Burton (Eds.), *Black women's mental health: Balancing strength and vulnerability* (pp. 43–55). State University of New York Press.

Weaver, M., & Sullins, J. (2022). The relationship between adverse childhood experience, guilt proneness, and shame-proneness: An exploratory investigation. *Modern Psychological Studies, 27*(1), Article 10.

Weber, M. C., Smith, A. J., Jones, R. T., Holmes, G. A., Johnson, A. L., Patrick, R. N., Alexander, M. D., Miyazaki, Y., Wright, H., & Ehman, A. C. (2023). Moral injury and psychosocial functioning in health care workers during the COVID-19 pandemic. *Psychological Services, 20*(1), 19–29.

White, C. N., Swan, S., & Smith, B. (2023). Trauma, help-seeking, and the Strong Black Woman. *Journal of Black Psychology, 49*(4), 498–528. https://doi.org/10.1177/00957984231191859

Zerach, G., Ben-Yehuda, A., & Levi-Belz, Y. (2023). Pre-deployment aggressiveness, combat exposure and moral injury as contributors to posttraumatic stress symptoms among combatants: A two-year prospective study. *Journal of Psychiatric Research, 161*, 158–164. https://doi.org/10.1016/j.jpsychires.2023.03.015

Zerach, G., & Levi-Belz, Y. (2021). Letter to the editor: Moral injury: A new (old) challenge for world psychiatry. *Journal of Psychiatric Research, 143*, 599–601. https://doi.org/10.1016/j.jpsychires.2020.11.020

Zimmermann, P., Willmund, G., Alliger-Horn, C., & Rau, H. (2023). Moralische konflikte im rahmen militärischer traumatisierungen: Übersicht und kasuistik aus dem kontext von militär und einsatzkräften [Moral conflicts in the context of military traumatization: Overview and casuistry from the context of the military and emergency forces]. *Trauma & Gewalt, 17*(4), 312–321. https://doi.org/10.21706/tg-17-4-312

INDEX